Eventful Journeys

Elisabeth Winkler is a freelance journalist whose credits include *The Independent on Sunday, The Guardian, The Sunday Times Magazine, Marie Claire* and *Cosmopolitan.* Her US credits include *Lifestyles Magazine* and *Mothering.* She was the author of Earthmother, a weekly political column for *The Bristol Evening Post.* Much of her work has centred on people who have survived the extremes of human experience, as well as celebrity interviews with figures ranging from Boy George to Oliver Sacks. She has written extensively on the Holocaust and was a video interviewer for the Survivors of the Shoah Visual History Foundation, founded by Steven Spielberg.

Eventful Journeys

The Story of
Leah and Sigo Weber

As told to Elisabeth Winkler

Pomegranate
Books

First published in 2000 by Pomegranate Books

© 2000 Michael Weber

Designed by John Adler Associates
Produced by Brokenborough Publications
Printed in Great Britain

ISBN 1-84289-001-8

Pomegranate Books
3 Brynland Avenue, Bristol BS7 9DR, England
www.pomegranatebooks.co.uk

Contents

Preface

In the years between 1933, when Hitler assumed power in Germany, and the outbreak of World War II, several hundred thousand Jewish people left mainland Europe seeking sanctuary. They are survivors. Whilst their experiences do not compare in severity to those left behind, their stories nonetheless have their own drama: upheaval, the loss of home and country, flight to unexpected places, new languages to learn and new cultures to adopt, years of uncertainty, the tragedy of friends and family left behind and the grief when the terrible news of their fate eventually emerged. This book is about such experiences.

Leah and Sigo Weber were fortunate enough to escape the net of Nazi terror in time and avoid the worst of what was to befall many millions of others. They were to undertake two basic journeys. One was a journey of escape, the other a journey to the promise of a better future. Through their determination to prevail, people such as Leah and Sigo were able to transcend their pain and build a future from modest beginnings. Their eventual success was the result of effort, courage and the desire to prioritise their humanity, underpinned of course by good fortune.

Eventful Journeys is a document detailing the experience of a generation of innocent people who suddenly found themselves caught in a web of political terror and social ostracism. It also serves as a resource for future generations of Jewish people to know something of what their forebears had to go through. In this respect, Sandy Weber, the daughter-in-law of Leah and Sigo, was an important moving force in the creation of this book. Because it is a story she wanted her sons and their children's children to know.

John Adler
Publisher

PART I - Early Years
Leah (Ost) Weber

My name is Leah. I was born on the 3rd July 1917 in the city of Moravska Ostrava. Today it is called by its Czech name, Ostrava. Before the Nazi occupation, about twenty per cent of its 120,000 inhabitants were Jewish.

There was not one street where I did not have family or friends. When I was a teenager I used to complain: "I cannot go anywhere without being spied on!"

But knowing people and being known also gave me a feeling of strength and safety. I have only been back to Ostrava once since I left. Now only a small handful of Jews remain and all of them are strangers.

I was the third of four children. My brother, Salo, was six years older; my sister, Erna, was older than me by two years and my little sister, Hilde, was born five years after me.

My father had two shops that sold men's clothing. My mother sometimes helped him but mostly she was at home. She ran a beautiful household with good continental Jewish food.

Friday nights were always an occasion with friends and relatives visiting. My mother's uncle came twice a year from Poland with a horse and cart to collect cast-off clothes for poor Polish Jews. He always headed for our house on Friday nights because he knew he would be well fed.

"Resi," he would say, "your *challahs* shine like the sun!"

My mother's name was Teresa and her maiden name was Schlachet. My mother's paternal family came from Poland where her father was a dairy wholesaler. Every morning he would collect produce from the neighbouring farms and sell them at the market.

My mother was born in Ostrava, as was her mother, Fani Schlachet. I did not know my grandfather, who died before I was born. My mother had four sisters and two brothers, so I was surrounded by loving aunts and uncles. My father, Moshe Ost, came from Rozvadov in Poland. His family were quite well off as they had a farm and a village shop. But he was not as well educated as my mother because he had left school early. This came about because when he was thirteen, his father was thrown from a horse and killed. According to Jewish custom, his widow married her dead husband's brother. But Moshe didn't get on with his new stepfather and after his *barmitzvah* he ran away from home and school. Moshe went to stay with an uncle in Germany who wanted him to join his business. But my father said no and came to Ostrava to try to set up his own business. My parents were probably introduced to each other through a *shadchen* and Moshe opened his first shop with the wedding dowry.

I didn't know my father terribly well because he travelled a lot from factory to factory buying clothes and shoes for his shops. A smallish man with fair hair and blue eyes, he was very good-natured - if I wanted a small luxury, he was the one to ask.

I never met my father's mother but my mother used to write regularly in German - using Hebrew lettering - because this was the only way her mother-in-law could understand. I still remember the address on the envelope to my grandmother: Mala Polska (small Poland) Nad Sasem (above river).

Like many women, my mother had more time for us than my

father. She was very kind with a sympathetic ear and my cousins would often come to her when they needed help or advice.

Our apartment was in a big block of flats. On the fifth floor were the laundry rooms where clothes and linen were washed and hung to dry. On washing day the maid (my mother always had someone to help her) would struggle up the stairs with a big washing basket - there was no lift.

Every flat had its own lavatory. When I was about four, we had a proper bathroom built. Up until then we used a big portable bath heated with the embers from the kitchen stove.

*

When I remember the past, I always see myself in the kitchen - it was the heart of our home. We had most of our meals round a big wooden table and I would spend hours talking to my mother as she baked and cooked. In the summer she used the gas stove because the coal stove made the flat too hot - but she always used the coal stove for baking her marvellous *challahs* and cakes.

One day when she was baking, I said,

"Mamma, I've got to have a white dress."

I was six years old and President Tomas Garrick Maseryk was coming to our school. He was a hero because he had introduced laws to Czechoslovakia making everyone equal.

That day the teacher had asked for a volunteer to present him with a bouquet of flowers.

"Has anyone got a white dress?" asked the teacher. If you did, you got the job.

Up shot my arm. I did not have one but I felt sure that my mother would help me.

"You are spoilt," laughed my mother, "I can't afford that."

But she bought me a dress from a department store. Presenting the bouquet filled me with excitement and pride. He was a tall, good-looking man and for years I'd tell people, "I met the President."

❡

From an early age I was interested in clothes and how they were made. I would give a fashion report to my mother.

"They are wearing sailor tops with a white button-on blouse and navy blouses with a sailor collar and navy blue coats" and "a girl at school has a pleated skirt - can I have one?"

Eventually I learned to make one. Twice a year a dressmaker would come to our home and stayed for a week. She repaired and altered our clothes and linen.

❡

Ostrava was a well-to-do, industrial town known for its good food and entertainment. We locals called it Little Paris because it was so fashionable. Jews were mostly middle class academics or retailers. The department stores were mainly owned by Jews and the biggest steel works in Czechoslovakia belonged to the Rothschilds.

Ostrava was only twenty minutes away by car from the border and before 1939, German tourists would visit Little Paris for weekends.

The city boasted two theatres, one German and one Czech, and we often saw productions which were not even showing in Prague. I loved the theatre, the opera and the ballet and I would go with my school, standing room only. Once the theatre was so packed during a Goethe production that I fainted. Or I would borrow my mother's subscription card and sprawl luxuriously in her seat. If I went with my mother, we would dress up in our best.

My father liked operetta. He had a musical ear and when he got home he would sing all the songs from memory. He was also an excellent skater and in the winter, when the tennis courts were converted to an ice-rink, he took me skating. But when I was eight I would go after school with my friends.

I read any new novel, more often in German than Czech, although I was fluent in both. Our next door neighbour was a Czech patriot and school teacher - if she heard me making a mistake, she would call on me at home to correct me.

ψ

Our apartment was too small for a piano. Only my big brother Salo learned a musical instrument but he gave up the violin because we girls teased him.

Salo really wanted to be a footballer. I used to smuggle his boots out of the apartment and he'd get a smack from my father for neglecting his studies. Salo didn't like school. My father wanted him to take over his shop but that was too middle-of-the-road for my brother. As soon as he was fourteen, Salo found himself a position with an exclusive men's shop to be trained as a shop assistant. He was a hot-headed young man with a mind of his own.

ψ

The family belonged to an Orthodox synagogue but as I was in the choir of the Liberal Synagogue. Very often I sung there on a Friday night or Saturday.

My parents were observant Jews and my mother ran a kosher household. She would not have dared do otherwise or my maternal grandmother would have refused to eat there. I was especially close to my grandmother, Fani (Francis) Schlachet, and visited her nearly every day. Of all the relatives, she singled me out. She had a two-bedroom flat about five minutes' walk from our apartment. My greatest treat was to join her after school for hot milk and rusks which she ate because of her poor digestion.

I had a lot to say to her and I felt at home with her even though she was formal. She never cuddled us and when we met I would kiss her hand and she would peck my forehead. But we felt loved by her. Once I repeated a slightly risqué joke that my father had told us. I didn't even understand it but I thought it would make her laugh as much as it did my parents. My poor father really copped it.

"How could you tell such a story in front of the children?" she said to him sternly.

She didn't go to synagogue but went to services in a *stiebl* in a religious man's house. Every *Yom Kippur* my mother would send us there with lemon and sugar in case she felt faint. But she would never take it.

My grandmother died when I was twelve. When I saw her in her coffin, I was shocked. It was the first time I had seen her without her *sheitl*. I knew her with dark hair and here was a shrivelled old lady with grey hair. When she was alive, her personality was so big that I had not noticed that she herself was small.

My mother's sister, Tante Helena, had eight children, all active Zionists and all older than I. Czechoslovakia was Jewish conscious and Ostrova was a centre for Zionist activity. The President of the Zionist Federation came from my home town as did many other members of the foundation movement.

Tante Helena's eldest boy was Shlomo Rosen (Shlomo was my grandfather's name and a family name). After his matriculation in 1922, he went to Palestine and helped found the Kibbutz Sarid, one of the first socialist *kibbutzim*. After learning Yiddish, he was sent to Poland to organise *aliyah* for Polish Jews and help them settle in Palestine. All eight cousins and their parents were safely in Palestine by the time that Hitler marched in, thanks to Shlomo.

My cousins were very aware of poverty in Czechoslovakia and felt strongly about the second-class position of Jews. Ever since I was little, I was inspired by my cousins and at the age of seven I joined the Zionist Youth Movement. One of Shlomo's sisters, Lina, was a leader in the Zionist Youth Movement. In those days I was called by my first name which was also Lina.

"Come and join us, you will have a great time," Lina said one day.

And I did. It was one of the happiest periods of my life. I had freedom, fun and friends. My mother was happy to let me go off for the weekend because she knew that I would be with my big cousins. On Saturdays we would meet for lectures, Hebrew classes (which I promptly forgot), games and songs. On Sundays we would go for country walks. We would go hiking - even in the winter, learning to survive in preparation for the deserts of Palestine.

I was fired up, inspired by the idea of a place where Jews were free. I was determined to join my big cousin Shlomo in Palestine and help create the country of our dreams.

During the early Thirties we still felt secure. We all thought that Czechoslovakia would go to war against Germany. Preparations had been made for years - for instance there was compulsory nursing training at school. At first my parents would not hear of me going to Palestine. But as the decade progressed they could see that trouble was brewing in Europe and they supported me. Eventually I did not think of anything but how to get out.

Czechoslovakia had laws against anti-Semitism and we felt sure that President Masaryk would not allow fascist ideas to take root in our country. But the truth is that, although anti-Semitism did not exist officially, it was there under the surface, in people's minds and hearts.

Once when I was eight or nine, my big brother saw someone he knew torment an old Jew by pulling his *kaftan*. Salo was a conscious Jew who would never let me, or anyone he cared about be pushed around.

"Stop it," shouted Salo.

There was a fight and my brother gave the boy a bleeding nose. The boy's mother took Salo to court.

"Would you ever do that again?" asked the judge to my brother.

"Yes," said my brother.

"Good for you," said the judge.

My brother was not only let off but commended thanks to the judge's support of minority rights.

I could have gone to a Jewish school because there was a top one in Ostrava but my mother refused. She had been a pupil there. Once when it had been snowing hard, she had arrived an hour late by horse and cart. Her teacher had smacked her and made her stand, wet and shivering, in the corridor as a punishment. This teacher was now the headmaster.

"I am not sending you to a school with such a cruel man," she said.

Instead I went to a Czech elementary school for five years and then to a German gymnasium. It was a means-tested scholarship school.

I did not come up against overt racism - at our school there were twenty percent Jewish girls and no one would have dared to take us on. But the signs were beginning, subtly. The German girls at school started wearing white knee socks in the Nazi fashion. I used to have a lot of non-Jewish friends but slowly we grew more distant. I didn't trust them any more and they stopped inviting me to their houses. I think they were pushed by their parents and probably told not to associate with Jews. There was a feeling that something bad was coming - my happy, carefree days felt like a thing of the past.

I was bright and would have gone to university - probably to study medicine - but the threat of Nazi hostility made my mother change her mind. She didn't think I could count on finishing my studies with Hitler on the doorstep.

"You have to be able to use your hands to make a living."

So when I was sixteen, I left school and went to a college for domestic science to learn dressmaking.

Erna lived at home until she got married. She left school at fourteen and became a dressmaker's apprentice. After three years qualification, she set up her own business in a rented room making dresses for Ostrava ladies.

My older sister grew into a vivacious young woman. She was pretty with piercing blue eyes and dark wavy hair and always surrounded by boyfriends and girlfriends. She loved to go dancing - the tango, the foxtrot - and that's how she met Stana. Erna loved him but although his mother was Jewish, he had been brought up a Catholic and my parents would not dream of letting her marry him.

We three girls shared a bedroom and I would hear her crying at night.

"I think you should be allowed to marry him," I told her.

I liked Stana because he was always friendly and good fun. I was cross with my parents for being so stubborn.

Once when discussing my dream of going to Palestine, my mother had confessed:

"When I was a young woman I had wanted to go to America."

Apparently she had been engaged to a young man and he had wanted to emigrate but my grandmother wouldn't hear of her going. So my mother abandoned her dreams and married my father instead.

"You can't always get what you want in life," my mother said.

✣

I was the only one on Erna's side. Our brother Salo did not like us going out with non-Jews. He had once told Stana,

"If you go near her I'll beat you up."

When he was rejected, Stana tried to commit suicide. His parents begged mine to relent. Perhaps my parents would have done but my grandmother was adamant.

"If Erna marries that boy, I will sit *shivah*," said my grandmother.

Like many traditional Jews, a child marrying out of the faith was equivalent to a death. What can you do? Jews can be as bigoted as everyone else. Erna couldn't see a way out. It was so ingrained in us to do as we were told and she didn't have a fighting spirit.

A year after breaking up with Stana, she married a Jewish man, Oscar Fränkel. He was a good-looking decent man and he worked as a department store assistant. But I resented him because he was not Stana.

PART I - Early Years
Sigo Vitezslav Weber

My name is Sigo. I was born on the 20th March 1915 in the village of Lanczany on the river Vistula. Then it was in the Austrian-Hungarian Empire but, after the Great War ended in 1918, it became Polish. Auschwitz was the nearest big town.

None of my grandparents were alive when I was born. My maternal grandparents had an inn on the river Vistula. My mother inherited it and that is where I was born. The river was used for floating timber downstream and the people riding the logs would stay overnight at the inn.

This is where my mother Malka Farber grew up. She was born late in her father's life, during his second marriage, so that by the time I was born my cousins were already grown-up. As was the custom, her marriage to my father was probably arranged because Jews lived so far apart from each other. The *shadchen* would travel miles between villages on foot or horseback, bringing news from one family to another.

The newly married couple lived at the inn. She had her first child when she was thirty and within four years she and my father had three sons, Jacob, Max and myself. When I was three, we moved to Teschen.

Tesin is the Czech spelling - in German it is Teschen and Cieszyn in Polish. Teschen was in Eastern Silesia and was claimed by both the Czechs and Poles after the break-up of the Austro-Hungarian

Empire. The dispute was eventually resolved by dividing the area between the two claimants with the river Olsa as the borderline.

The older and historic part of Teschen became Polish, while the smaller part (where we lived) with its important railway junction, became part of Czechoslovakia. In Teschen there were two bridges over the river Olsa and people living locally were issued with passes to enable them to cross freely between the two countries.

My father's name was Aharon but my mother called him Arnold. I believe his family came originally from Teschen because his two elder brothers, Uncles Rudolph and Bernard, retired cattle and horse dealers lived there. After the partition, their homes were on the Polish side. Mother's two other brothers, Joseph and Sigmund, also lived on the Polish side, two short train journeys away inland in Polish Silesia.

Smuggling was rife in both directions; food was cheaper in Poland while many manufactured goods were cheaper on the Czech side.

The railway was the centre of everything because it brought life and work to the area. The station was only a seven-minute walk from our house - you could hear the trains at night.

We lived in Svibice, a suburb of Teschen. My parents kept a general store where they weighed out all the goods like flour, rice, salt or sugar from big sacks. Eggs, butter or vegetables were on sale at a twice-weekly market. Many produced their own, so my parents did not stock those. A lot was given on credit because people were poor - it was a hard living but that was normal.

We never went hungry but by the standards of the time and our area, we were considered well to do. We had two adjoining two-storey houses with about a dozen tenants. We lived on the second floor of one and the rest was let as apartments. It sounds grand but in those days a tenants' protection law kept the rents low. So, being a landlord was not a great income.

If I were to take you into my home, you would enter by the front door into the communal hall. A wide staircase separated it with apartments on either side. Downstairs led to the cellars where every tenant had a portion to store coal, potatoes and apples imbedded in straw to keep them safe from the frost during winter.

A big room on the ground floor was converted into the shop with a shop window and its own separate entrance. At the back of the house was a yard where every family had a storage shed, and behind that, a garden allotment for growing vegetables.

The house had a roof made of copper sheeting and was rendered on the outside. I still remember young children licking bits of mortar that had flaked away. Later, when I was at medical school, I realised that was probably how they got calcium in their diet from the lime in the mortar.

About half the houses in the village had an outside toilet but ours was inside because the house had been built at the beginning of the twentieth century. In my teens, we were amongst the first in the village to get a bathroom and water heater. Before then Nana would heat up a tin bath once a week in the kitchen with water boiled on the coal fired stove.

Nana was like a second mother to me. She was a servant who couldn't read or write but she was like a member of our family. As far as I know she did not suffer in the war, as she was a Catholic. After the war my brothers made sure that she was looked after and she lived in our flat where she died, a few years after the 1939-45 war. I last saw her in 1947, a happy and very sad visit.

Washing day was a big day. Clothes were cleaned with soap and a washing board in a giant tub. The laundry was pegged up in the yard, after which it was either ironed or mangled to soften it. If it rained, clothes could be dried in the attic, which was divided by slatted fences for each tenant.

We never went on family holidays and the first time my father took a break was after his heart attack (when I was fourteen) and he went to Marienbad for health reasons. We boys were sometimes sent during our summer holidays to family in Poland or friends in Czechoslovakia.

I lived in that house until I left for university in Brno at the age of 19 and then I would return for the long vacations.

ᶋ

My parents had grown up under the influence of the Emancipation. They were modern, influenced by the liberal movement in Germany. They loved the Austrian-Hapsburg royal family, German culture and read German newspapers. The Empire ended with the defeat of Austria-Hungary and the country my parents lived in now belonged to Czechoslovakia. Yet culturally they were really German, a tolerated minority.

Judaism was their religion that they observed reasonably. Although they knew Yiddish, they spoke to us in German. We boys did not speak Yiddish but we understood some of it.

"Our children don't "yiddle" - they speak good German," they would say.

ᶋ

My father was a good-looking man, tall by the standards of the day. Every Sunday he went to a cafe house to play Taroque, a Central European card game.

My mother didn't exactly follow fashion but she dressed well and bought material to be made up by the local seamstress. My mother did everything very fast and efficiently. She was the brain in the family. Businessmen would seek her advice.

Mother did all he cooking with Nana helping - nothing elaborate but good Jewish cooking. Nearly every Friday night we had chicken. This was quite a luxury - chickens were kept for laying, not eating, like they are today. My mother used the chicken or goose fat for *schmaltz* and also made boiled beef and tasty soup. Nothing was wasted - the goose feathers were used to make the family's duvets.

On *Shabbat*, the candles were lit on the heavy oak dining table and my father made a *brocha*. But we were not *frum* - the shop stayed open on Saturday. My father used to pray with *tefillin* but we boys didn't and eventually he gave up. We had blue crockery for dairy and red for *fleishig*. My parents did not eat *tref* but we boys ate anything outside the home. But later, at university, I became a more conscious Jew and I avoided obvious *tref*.

ψ

Svibice had about three or four Jewish families, a barber, a publican, a cattle dealer and a hairdresser. We were not particularly close and I grew up with mostly non-Jewish friends.

Three times a year we would go to synagogue in Teschen, for the two days of *Rosh Hashana* and one of *Yom Kippur*. There were several synagogues in Teschen. Most of Jewish life was on the Polish side and it was only later that we attended the synagogue on the Czech side.

The one we attended on the Polish side was purpose built before the Great War, a bit churchy with a balcony for the ladies. It was not strictly orthodox - there were no special *Cohanim* blessings and the organ was not played on Saturdays. The prayers were all in *Ivrit* (Ashkenazi Hebrew) but the sermon was in German.

Quite a few of the congregation, like my parents, would carry on working on *Shabbat*. The one concession my father made was not to smoke on *Shabbat*. (Talking about smoking, sometimes my mother would have a cigar, on the odd evening).

We didn't go to Sunday school but every week a pious man we called Uncle Schanzer would come to the house and give us individual lessons in Hebrew. We were not nice boys, we would run away when it was our time to be taught. As my *barmitzvah* grew closer, I studied with a semi-retired cantor from a synagogue in Teschen.

On the day of my *barmitzvah* in 1928 we walked from home in our Shabbat best and arrived at the synagogue on the Polish side of Teschen. The cantor steered me through my big day as I read *Maftir*.

In those days *barmitzvahs* were quiet affairs. There was a *kiddush* afterwards and, once back at home, I was given my first wristwatch - a precious, expensive thing.

When I was home from university, I would suggest going on a Saturday with my father to synagogue - it pleased him to arrive with his grown-up student son. By this time, his heart was bad and the walk that used to take ten minutes now took twice as long.

My earliest memory is concentrating on pulling an embroidery thread through paper at kindergarten when I was three years old. Proper school started at six. I was a bright kid, often top of the class. I went to elementary school in German and at eleven, I attended a Czech grammar state school or gymnasium. My best language became Czech and German became my second language.

I was a keen sportsman from an early age. I played tennis, table tennis, volley ball and soccer competitively, as well as ice-skating and skiing. Once a week we had a soccer match in an organised competition. When I was little I improvised a pair of skis with two slats from a wooden barrel and would ski down the little hill at the back of our house. When I was about sixteen I used to borrow Jacob's old skis and go skiing in the nearby Beskyd mountains, a few stops away by train.

At German elementary school I was amongst the star pupils. When it was clear at my Czech grammar school that I had a good academic brain, my parents sent me to university.

My brothers were also bright but I was the only one to go to university - perhaps as the youngest I was a bit spoilt. In those days university was rare and costly since it required living away from home.

Jacob and Max left school at fourteen and fifteen respectively. Jacob continued in a business college for another two years. Both my brothers served an apprenticeship in the retail trade then later became representatives for factories and travelled away from home a lot. It was during the Depression and they had a hard time.

∿

Anti-Semitism was illegal in Czechoslovakia and the rights of minorities were safeguarded. State schools existed for minorities in their own language, including a Hebrew grammar state school in the eastern part of Czechoslovakia.

That did not stop me being called a "dirty Jew" on a couple of occasions. My relationship with people my own age, at school or sport was good. I could look after myself - I was sporty and handy with my fists.

After Hitler came to power in Germany in 1933, there were no posters or slogans because this was Czechoslovakia. But change was in the air. Certain Czech school friends began to distance themselves. It wasn't hate - they were playing safe, I suppose.

One of my professors, an enlightened man, suggested that I study mining engineering and law because he felt I had the ability.

"Do you really think the local coal-owner would give me a job as a Jew?" I asked.

He patted my shoulder, silently, but with, I felt, genuine sympathy.

∿

At grammar school I was a good Czech and I belonged to a strongly nationalist sports club. But even though I was not an observant Jew, I was seen as different. My eyes opened to anti-Semitism and I decided to join the Maccabi Sports Club where I felt I belonged.

I became acquainted with the ideas of Zionism and I began to feel that this was the way forward. My parents were not pleased at first. The idea that a Czech citizen would want to live in a strange country did not appeal. They believed that our loyalty should be towards the country where we lived.

My eldest brother Jacob was not exactly a Zionist but he felt Jewish. In contrast, Max was not a happy Jew. He regretted his religion and culture and for some time identified as strongly German.

Our family was very much a democracy - we discussed everything together. We didn't fall out over it because we loved each other and accepted each other's differences. Gradually my parents realised that the world was changing and they supported my growing interest in Zionism.

PART II - Pre-War
Leah Weber

I n 1933, when I was sixteen, I attended college of domestic science for three years where I concentrated on dressmaking. I was very quick at picking things up and I would have been entitled to become a teacher but this was not my plan.

In 1936 I started working as a dressmaker in an exclusive salon. The pay was practically nothing - you were supposed to feel honoured to be taken on by the boss, Madame Biederer. I think one of my relatives who had her clothes made there must have put in a good word for me. The clientele were prosperous and mainly Jewish.

First I learnt the basics, finishing seams and buttons. After a year I had to make a dress for my exams. It was a green chiffon cocktail dress made to my measurements. The boss, a perfectionist, fitted it and I passed with honours. I hardly ever wore it but it was probably the best made dress that I have ever possessed.

Madame Biederer had a salon in her spacious apartment. In another room was the workshop where about six of us worked from eight in the morning to six at night. Her ex-husband had a man's salon in a shop called *Immer Elegante* - always elegant.

✢

I didn't have much spare time but I always had a friend from my Zionist group to go out with. We would meet up with our other friends in a cafe house and talk. At the weekends we would go hiking and skiing in the Beskyd mountains, about three quarters of an hour's journey by train.

Nazism was creeping in - you would hear people refer to "those Jews". One of the girls in my workshop was scathing when Madame Biederer angled for a meeting with the girl's recently widowed father.

"Silly woman," said the girl. "Doesn't she know that my father would never go out with a Jew?"

"That's your father's loss," I retorted.

I didn't like Madame Biederer but I found such remarks offensive. We Zionists never let rude remarks go without answering back.

It was around this time that I changed my name from Lina to Leah. Leah was my Hebrew name and how my grandmother called me. It was the fashion amongst Zionists to be as Israeli as possible. So I became Leah.

On the first of May I would march with the Socialist Youth movement on the streets of Ostrava with our red flags flying. Some of the girls were in their fur coats striding alongside the children of miners. But our beliefs were sincere.

I knew quite a few communists. One chap tried to recruit me to open a branch for communist youth. His entire family were communists, intellectual people with substantial means. We called them salon communists because they preached from the comfort of their armchairs. He was sincere but I didn't like the offer because everything had to be done on the quiet. It felt too underhand.

In 1938, I left Madame Biederer's Salon and travelled to Karlsbad, the spa town, where the Zionist Federation was helping train young people for Palestine. We did *Hachshara* - where we learned how to live together as a group and do practical, manual work like chopping wood and planting seeds. We were inspired, prepared to give up being undergraduates in order to learn to live on the land.

The *Chalutz* movement was run on experimental socialist ideas. For instance you were expected to share everything. When a group of young people came from Kapato in Russia, they were so poor that they had no shoes when they were children.

"You don't mind if I take this jumper?" one would ask.

"Go on, take it," I'd say, feeling a glow of goodness.

I knew very well that I would get a new one when I got home.

Some of our fine ideals did not take into account human nature. For instance the idea that everyone is equal.

"But some are more equal than others," we would mutter when someone threw their weight around.

I no longer worked as a dressmaker - that was considered too posh - instead I packed eggs in a factory. It was boring but well paid and I felt very self-righteous.

"This is how life should be run," I thought.

※

I enjoyed my nine months in Karlsbad, the companionship of being with a group of twenty or so like-minded people and we all got on well. One of my weekend duties was to talk to Jewish communities in Sudeten and give them information about Zionism. I liked communicating and I was quite a success, helping gather groups together that then went to Palestine. But my mother had a mild heart attack and wrote asking me to return. I was ready to come home.

※

In 1938 after the Munich Agreement, the Germans occupied Sudetenland and we talked more seriously about getting out. I was one of the first to gain a certificate for Palestine from the Zionist Federation but, as I also had a valid passport, I was asked by the Federation to give my certificate to someone else and travel instead to Britain. The plan was that I would travel with my *Blauweiss* (blue-white) group from Ostrava to England. I would continue my training there with a *Hachshara* group and re-apply for a certificate for Palestine.

My departure happened very quickly. A leader in the Zionist Youth movement said to me,

"If you want to go, then you have to get out now. Pack a suitcase with all your clothes. But Leah, don't take anything fancy - you won't need it."

My mother wanted to give me elaborate household goods, like candlesticks or a good set of knives, but I refused.

"Who needs it?" I said.

As I went round saying my goodbyes to my relatives, I would say,

"I'll be back soon."

Our daily life had been turned upside down and everything was chaotic but we felt that this was a temporary situation, which would soon be resolved. We didn't imagine that things could get worse.

There were no big send-offs, no official goodbyes - we kept it low key. You were considered lucky to have somewhere to go and people wished you all the best as you disappeared into your new life.

"I'll see you," I would say casually as I left.

One day I met my Czech neighbour on the stairs.

"I hear you are off to Britain. Well, don't marry one of those English Lords," she said.

"Oh, they are queuing up for me," I wisecracked.

I made light of my situation - no one really knew what lay ahead.

I said goodbye to Erna. She would have liked to go to Palestine but her husband Oscar was not ready to leave. My mother was also held back - my father was a very sick man and she wouldn't dream of leaving him. But she didn't mind me going - she was only too happy that I was getting out.

We were told to travel by train to Prague. At the station I noticed that my mother had something in her hand.

"I don't need pearls!" I said as she pressed her precious necklace into my hand. "You keep them."

She did and I never regretted that. During the war I often thought,

"Maybe she can sell the pearls to buy food."

Other groups joined us in the hotel including a student group from the University of Brno. I had a boyfriend in Prague but I dropped him because, as soon as I saw Sigo, it was love at first sight - I really fell for him. I thought he was charming and clever.

We would walk round Prague together, talking. We clicked right from the start - we could talk to each other and when he smiled, I felt good. Sigo met my little sister Hilde who was with a Zionist children's group in Prague at the time. Before she left for Palestine I bought her an ice cream as a treat and Sigo petted her as if she was a little kid rather than fifteen. I saw Hilde off on her train.

"See you soon," I said.

I thought it was only a matter of time before I would join her in Palestine.

PART II - Pre-War
Sigo Weber

In 1934, when I was nineteen, I went to university to become a doctor. In those days any sensible Jewish man who wanted to succeed chose either medicine or law, a profession where one was not dependent on being an employee. I preferred medicine because it meant an extra year at university.

Did I enjoy my university years? The answer is yes and no. I enjoyed the successes in my work and the social life. But the 1929 Wall Street crash had resulted in a worldwide economic depression, at its deepest in Czechoslovakia at this time. My means were limited and I had to manage on little rather than ask for more support from my parents. Life in a capital city like Brno was expensive. I went to the odd theatre or opera production but that usually meant missing a meal.

At university I became involved in student politics and was elected to the council of the Medical Students Association. I stood as a Jew. This was possible because citizenship and nationality were considered two separate things in Czechoslovakia.

For instance in the census, my parents and I would have registered our citizenship as Czech. But they would have registered their nationality as German and I registered mine as Jewish.

I was active in *Jüdisch Akademische Lese Und Rede Halle*. This translates as the 'Jewish Academic Reading and Debating Hall'. It was a Jewish student fraternity founded well before the First World

War and I served for one year as president.

Once a week we had meeting or lectures to raise our Jewish aware-ness. In my time *Halle* was strongly Zionist. To be consciously Jewish it was not necessary to attend synagogue but it was important to stand up for being a Jew.

As Hitler's power grew and with it, the dangers to Germany's neighbours, I followed the news in the papers and every evening when I got back to my digs, I would sit and listen on my crystal radio for the latest developments. Like many, I hoped that Britain and France would come to the aid of Czechoslovakia against Hitler.

I spent the long summer holidays at home - I would read, study, or play sport competitively including soccer, tennis, skiing, volley-ball and table tennis.

In September 1938 I was due to go back to medical school for my fifth and final year when we heard that the Munich agreement had been signed.

The whole atmosphere suddenly changed. Britain and France had acceded to Hitler's demand for the immediate occupation of the predominantly German-speaking Sudentenland, in western Czecho-slovakia. One could hear remarks like:

"Chamberlain the Jew betrayed us."

I was shocked but at the same time it wasn't entirely unexpected. Anti-Semitism has always been a useful diversion from people's own *tsorres*, or troubles.

As a result of the Munich agreement, Poland occupied the Czech part of Eastern Silesia and overnight I turned into a Polish citizen.

I happened to be in Teschen to witness the arrival of the Polish army. We stood silently as several hundred Polish soldiers crossed the bridge on foot and watched as Czech officers handed over Teschen to Polish officers.

I did not expect this deal to directly impact my life. But when I returned to university to inscribe for my final year, I was told that the university could not accept my papers because I was no longer Czech but a Pole. No one dared say it was because I was a Polish Jew - but Christian students from the same area (now occupied by Poland) had no difficulty continuing their medical studies.

I resubmitted my documents repeatedly but to no avail.

I approached the president of the Medical Student Association. "Can you do anything for me?" I asked.

"I've done everything I can," he said.

A sympathetic man, he had already tried to intervene on behalf of other Jewish colleagues but with no success. He was a Christian Democrat but I learnt early that labels do not count. On the student council, there were communists who were anti-Semites and capitalists who were not. There is good and bad on all sides.

I learnt that it was the Dean of the Medical Faculty who had decided not to accept Jews from the territory now under Polish occupation.

My situation shocked me. Here I was, a man who had studied four years to be a doctor, when suddenly I was robbed of my future. For me, this is when the war began.

About this time someone approached me from the *Hechalutz*, a Zionist pioneering movement which tilted towards socialism. We *Halle* students were invited to join them in *hachshara* in Britain - to learn how to farm in preparation for going to Palestine. I couldn't carry on with my studies and this was a chance to get out, in line with my Zionists views. I took it.

By January 1939 I was ready to leave. I took some detective novels, clothes, a couple of suits and some photographs from home. I had the signet ring that my mother had made for me when I was a teenager and she also gave me the address of her much older brother, Simon Farber, in Buffalo, New York.

Although my mother cried as we said goodbye, there was no time for regret - the important thing was to take the opportunity to get out. The family was glad I was going into safety. That was the thinking of the time.

I was not sad to leave Czechoslovakia. My Zionist inclinations were a positive factor, the refusal to let me complete my studies was a negative one. I had been accepted for military service and was to report for duty on completion of my studies - but my Czech passport was stamped:

'Not valid for return to Czechoslovakia.'

I was not happy to leave my family but my thoughts were now full of plans for the future and that helped.

I arrived in Prague in the winter of 1938 with a group of about twenty participants, the majority from a Zionist youth movement. We stayed a few weeks while arrangements were finalised. It was a new experience to be in a beautiful city with a group of friends all pulling together. I was attracted by the idea of creating a Jewish state where everyone would be equal and we would be self-reliant.

The hotel was filled with different Zionists groups and Leah was one of the leaders of a *Chalutz* group. They were a lively group, with plenty of songs - very refreshing after the intellectualism of *Halle*.

Leah was very pretty and liked by everybody. We had a lot to talk about and were friendly from the first day. Right from the start her spirit attracted me.

Leah's family (Ost) before the War
Left to right (back row) Tante Anna and her husband Eugene, Moshe and Teresa (her father and mother), Onkel Hutterer, Onkel Samuel, Onkel Heinrich, Tante Regina, Onkel William (Wili) and Onkel Heinrich; *(front row)* Tante Ida, Tante Helena, Fani (her grandmother), Gusti (Augustina) and Tante Marie

Sigo's Parents
Malka and Aharon Weber

PLATE 1

Moravska Ostrava
Leah's home town in Czecholsovakia

Leah at a Reunion of her Hachshara Group (Moetzah of the Hechalutz), England 1941

PLATE 2

Erna Ost, Leah's Sister

Max Weber (Sigo's older brother) in Free Czech Army Uniform

Jacob (Kuba) Weber
Sigo's eldest brother

PLATE 3

The Webers with Michael at Witney

Judy and Michael in 1947

PLATE 4

The Weber Family in 1963/4

**Michael and Sandy Weber's
post-marriage reception** Sydney 1971

Robin and Judy Belcher's Wedding
London 1975

PLATE 5

GRANDSONS' BARMITZVAHS

Mark Weber 1985

David Weber 1990

PLATE 6

Jonathan Belcher 1994

Richard Belcher 1995

PLATE 7

Sigo and Leah's Diamond Wedding - Family Group
Left to right (back row) Jonathan, Robin and Richard Belcher; Martin, Bruno, Sylva and Philip Nägele; Mark, Sandy and David Weber; *(front row)* Judy, Sigo, Leah and Michael

Sigo and Leah with their Grandsons
Left to right Jonathan, Mark, Richard and David

PLATE 8

Leah's sister Hilde (Rachel), her husband Hans (Ze'ev) and children Gadi and Dalia (1961)

Batel, Leah and Salo (Shlomo) Ost with Leah Weber

Herta Foltyn, Sigo, Leah, Harry and Doris Gayst, Evzen Foltyn in Australia

PLATE 9

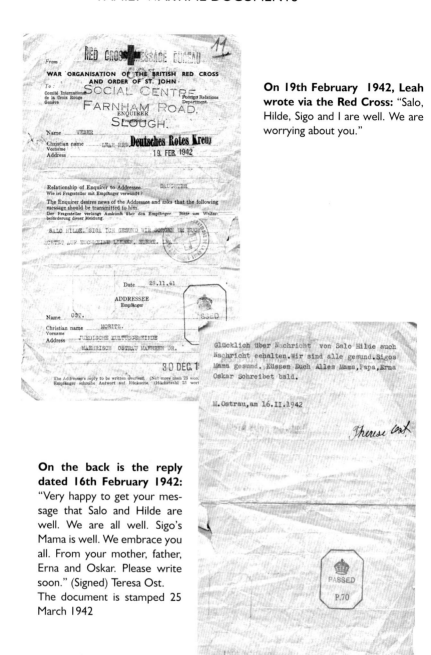

On 19th February 1942, Leah wrote via the Red Cross: "Salo, Hilde, Sigo and I are well. We are worrying about you."

On the back is the reply dated 16th February 1942: "Very happy to get your message that Salo and Hilde are well. We are all well. Sigo's Mama is well. We embrace you all. From your mother, father, Erna and Oskar. Please write soon." (Signed) Teresa Ost. The document is stamped 25 March 1942

PLATE 10

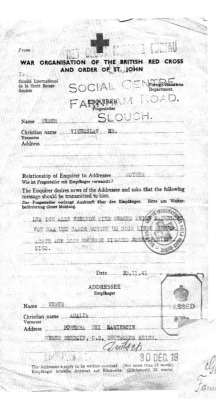

On 30th November 1941, Sigo wrote via the Red Cross: "Leah and I are well. Unfortunately, there is no news from Max and Jacob. We are worried about you. Please look after yourself and give my regards to Sigmund and Joseph?"

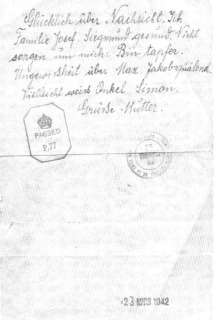

On the back is the reply stamped 23rd March 1942: "Happy about your message. I, myself and both Joseph and Sigmund's families are well. Don't worry about us - I am tough. I am very unhappy not knowing about Max and Jacob. Maybe Onkel Simon knows what is happening."

PLATE 11

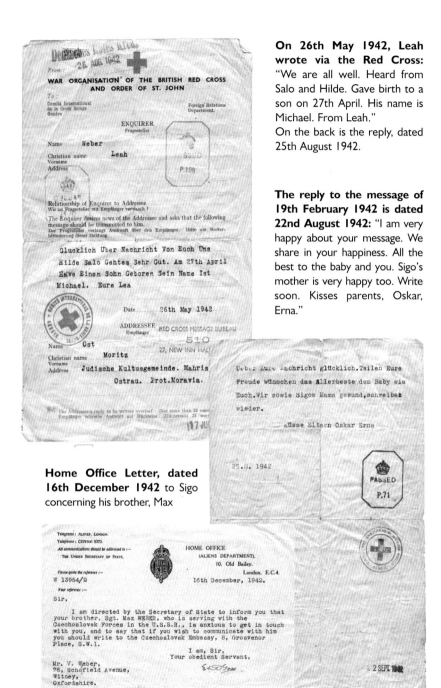

On 26th May 1942, Leah wrote via the Red Cross: "We are all well. Heard from Salo and Hilde. Gave birth to a son on 27th April. His name is Michael. From Leah."
On the back is the reply, dated 25th August 1942.

The reply to the message of 19th February 1942 is dated 22nd August 1942: "I am very happy about your message. We share in your happiness. All the best to the baby and you. Sigo's mother is very happy too. Write soon. Kisses parents, Oskar, Erna."

Home Office Letter, dated 16th December 1942 to Sigo concerning his brother, Max

PLATE 12

PART III - The War Years
Leah Weber

We were ready to leave for England. I wasn't sad to go because I was excited about what lay ahead. The train travelled through Europe. I was so sick on the Channel crossing from France to England - I am not a good sailor. We landed at Dover and went by train to London. At Victoria Station we were parcelled off in twos and threes and I went with a girl my age called Anne to an Anglo-Jewish family in Norwood. I did not know one word of English but luckily my friend did.

On the first morning the maid came into our bedroom bearing a tea tray. I had never drunk tea with milk in my life.

"Look, Anne," I said, "tell our hostess that I am not sick - I don't need tea. I am perfectly capable of drinking coffee."

The family laughed about this for days. Now, I prefer tea with milk.

Sigo would come to visit with Anna's husband - Anna had recently married before leaving Czechoslovakia. One day, shortly after our arrival in March 1939, we went to the capital's centre to visit the tourist attractions. We were in Trafalgar Square when a newsboy called out,

"Hitler invades Czechoslovakia."

We were stunned - it was terrible thinking of our families, trapped. But at the same time, we felt resigned and unsurprised by Czechoslovakia's lack of resistance.

When Britain declared war against Germany in the following September, on one level we were pleased because we thought that the British would beat the Germans quickly and we could go home. We never panicked - we were convinced that Britain could not lose. We were full of wishful and optimistic thinking.

It was important for me to be married. Sigo and I got on well, we wanted to be together and I had no doubt that he was the man for me. It wasn't a moral issue but I wanted to make things comfortable for my family back home. I wrote to my mother with the news and Erna went to visit Sigo's parents in Teschen. My mother wrote back saying that she was sending me wedding gifts in a crate including duvets and a wedding dress hand-made by Erna who was a fantastic dressmaker. I waited for the wedding crate but when it arrived, it was empty. Look, I never cared about material things - far worse things happened.

The parents of a friend kindly offered to have the wedding, complete with *chupah*, in their living room. On the fourteenth of December 1939, twenty of us crowded under the wedding canopy. I was very moved. Our Zionist organisation gave us money to pay the rabbi. Sigo handed him the envelope but the rabbi handed it back to me.

"Your wedding present," he said.

I was showered with presents: *Twenty Thousand Leagues Under the Sea* by Jules Verne; a wooden camel which I still have - personal presents which meant a lot. I got married with a borrowed ring in an old dress but it did not matter because Sigo and I were safe and free to make a life together.

After we were married, our farm suddenly become suspect - we were aliens too near the coast. Spies! The thought made us laugh. By this time, Sigo and I had moved to London, to a Czech hostel, so Sigo could get hospital treatment for his stomach ulcer.

We could have taken an allowance from a Czech Trust Fund and Sigo could have completed his medical training but we preferred to be independent. I rented a sewing machine and did repairs. Soon I had enough money to buy a second-hand machine. One friend tells another - I always had work.

Sigo was in hospital and I visited him every day. One day I went and found the landscape completely transformed. Where was the hospital?

"A direct hit," a man said.

There were people running about. I stopped another man.

"Where is everybody?" I asked.

At the enquiries station area, I was told,

"The patients were evacuated earlier this afternoon."

Sigo's and all the other wards had been taken by ambulance to Oxford just hours before a bomb landed on the hospital. To my relief Sigo got in touch by letter and I went to the police to get permission to go to Oxford. It was a miracle but, looking back, we took it in our stride. We had no choice.

We were quite blasé about the bombs –A few weeks previously I had been sitting on my bed at the *Hechalutz* hostel chatting with my friend Gretel when the air raid siren went off. We thought we were safe and just continued sitting there. Suddenly there was a loud cracking sound. The roof came crashing down but luckily we were on the ground floor. Gretel and I were buried under plaster and hit by bits of flying wood.

"Anyone there?" shouted the air-raid warden. "Don't worry, we'll get you out."

We had to be dug out but we were not hurt. Gretel and I were so pleased with ourselves for surviving that we spent our last half-crown on an ice cream at the Lyons Corner House.

Gretel now lives in Cricklewood and sometimes we remember our bravado. The sky in the East End of London was lit up at night with fires. It was horrific but somehow we got used to being bombed. The next morning, I'd see the damage caused - buildings no longer standing and people you knew no longer there. It's not that we had got used to it, but people were magnificent, sharing everything, having sing-songs in the air-raid shelters, being helpful. You would be surprised how it helps to know that you are not alone.

Some people were broken by the war but Sigo and I were young - we could take it. We were so young that life was more of an adventure than a horror. And we felt lucky that we were not locked up in a German camp.

Our new address was New Inn, Hall Street. We lived in the Czech hostel next door to some refugee offices. An English lady called Mrs. Seaward was doing full-time charity work on the refugee committee. When she heard that I could sew, she gave me work. Material was hard to come by so one would make a day dress out of an evening one. She had a beautiful country house and sometimes, if I had a lot of sewing to do, I stayed the night.

When I became pregnant in 1941, I was happy. Sigo and I were such optimists. We never thought we were poor. We had enough to eat and I could make do and mend. The war would end and soon we could be our own people again. I wasn't worried - we were well off. We felt rich, lucky that we were free to walk around.

I heard from my mother throughout the war. I received letters through the Red Cross, written in her own handwriting. There was only room for a few lines. I would get a message once a month that told me that they were still alive. Then in 1940, I heard that my father was sick with Parkinson's disease.

Oxford was quiet and safe. Apart from the black-outs, there were no signs of war. It was not blitzed and it had more theatre and concerts than in London. The provisional Czech government was based in Oxford and President Eduard Benes, the president of Czecho-slovakia was invited by Balliol College to give a lecture. He spoke in English so we had some trouble understanding him. But we were not the only ones.

"I never realised Czech sounded so much like our language," whispered an Englishman to me.

Our hostel received a visit from all the big shots, including the son of President Mazaryk. When we bombarded him with questions, he could only answer,

"What do you want of me? I am only my father's son."

Eventually we found a lovely big room under a sloping roof at the top of a house in Oxford. It had mice but we soon got rid of them. The house was in the middle of the city, surrounded by the colleges and near to the Czech hostel where we took our meals.

Sigo was still training but I was working so we could afford our new flat. In the evenings I read novels, like the latest Graham Greene, or we would socialise. We were happy. We had a lot of friends, some we see to this day - I have never lost a friend. We would often eat with our close friends Judith and Samuel Smith (previously Schmitt).

Mrs. Seaward was also sweet to me and bought half the layette for the new baby. I felt looked after and lucky. Sigo trained in Slough as an engineer draughtsman and I joined him for a few months. I was seven months pregnant when we returned to Oxford only to find that the Czech hostel could not take us. So there I was, seven months pregnant and homeless!

We were sent to the German hostel. The landlady came to the door and looked me up and down.

"How long have you been married?" she asked.

"Two years," I said.

"What does your husband do?" she asked.

"Medical student," I said.

"Please come in, Frau Doctor."

I have never graduated so fast up the social ladder - we dined out on that story for a long time.

❦

In 1942 my parents were taken to Theresienstadt which we knew to be a Jewish ghetto. At first I was upset but I comforted myself. It sounded as if normal life still went on because my mother worked as a nurse in the hospital and children went to school. Then she wrote to say that my father had died. I was not too despairing because I was convinced that I would see my mother again.

Sigo got a job in Witney which is just outside Oxford and just before Michael's birth we found a two-room flat with its own bathroom. This was luxury to us. In the middle of the night I woke up. Labour had started. I did not know what to expect, there were no female relatives to help and advise. We called the ambulance driver - he was very kind and took Sigo home in his own car. It was a long labour but I have good memories because the midwives were all so kind.

❦

Michael was born on the 27th April 1942. When the baby was put into my arms, I was thrilled. Once back in our flat I felt a tired and lost. Sigo was good but he had a job himself. I missed my family. When the baby cried, I cried. I didn't have a lot of strength and sometimes Gretel came to take Michael out for a walk in the pram. My mother wrote to say how thrilled they were that Michael was born and that Sigo's mother was happy too. As was the custom, everyone was thrilled that our first child was a boy.

❦

Although I sometimes felt alone, I was so convinced I would see my family soon. I never gave the alternative a thought.

I breast fed Michael for four months. I was small and skinny and as he put on weight, I lost it. The rations enabled me to get him

Cow and Gate orange or blackcurrant juice. He slept in a big washing basket until he was six months old and I had paid off the cot, five shillings a week. It's amazing what you can do when you have to. He was a very good baby, a sweet and lovely boy.

Although Witney was ten miles away from Oxford, people could jump on the bus and visit us. We kept the big bed with the iron bedstead and could put them up. We had soldiers visiting us from the Czech army and when my cousin Arthur had leave, he visited us too. Arthur was one of Shlomo's brothers, (the sons of one of my mother's sister Helena). He had joined the British forces from Palestine and been posted to Europe. Arthur would take Michael out in his pushchair. He was an active little boy - once Michael wriggled out of the straps, clambered on to an egg van and started pulling out the eggs. Eggs were so precious!

Shortly before the end of the war we moved to Cardiff. I did not know a soul. I put Michael in a kindergarten so that I had a few hours to work, dressmaking. He hated it - once when I picked him up he still had some potato in his mouth from lunch which he had pretended to swallow.

There were rumours that the war would end soon and we had the radio on non-stop. When the news came, it was marvellous. There were street parties everywhere. For the celebration on our street, I baked sponge cakes with a recipe from home. I felt part of my new community - I was always a good mixer.

Now we waited for news of our people. All we could hope for was that someone would come out alive. Every week I wrote to the Red Cross for news of my mother, of Erna and of Sigo's mother. We wrote to Theresienstadt and through every Jewish channel we could think of. If they were alive, they would surely make contact. We were always hopeful that we had overlooked some avenue and that we would hear something. But when I spoke to my relatives in Israel, where information was actively collected, there was no sign. Gradually I realised that there was nothing more to hope for. I had to assume the worst - that our dearest loved ones had not survived the war.

At this point we did not know how their lives had ended. Do you know the trauma of losing your family in this way? We learned bit by bit what had happened. We are still learning. People say, "Do you remember so and so? Well he...." And you hear some terrible story.

PART III - The War Years
Sigo Weber

We arrived at Victoria Station in London after crossing the channel. The journey from Prague was an ordinary train journey, travelling third class on wooden benches. But we were full of hope and expectancy. We were going to freedom.

The *Hechalutz* organisation had problems finding us accommodation. Temporary places were found for the girls with Jewish families and the boys went to a Salvation Army hostel for the night.

Refugees sometimes are inclined to feel sorry for themselves, which is understandable. Yet one should never forget the favours and assistance. I was grateful to the Salvation Army, to other non-Jewish organisations and to people encountered in my early years in the UK from whom I received friendship and assistance when I needed it.

Leah and her friend Anna Becker were staying with an Anglo-Jewish family in Norwood. A few days after our arrival in London, Anna's new husband, a friend of mine from university, and I decided to hitchhike to visit them. A man gave us a lift, and hearing from our accents that we were foreigners, drove us out of his way and across London to the address written down on a scrap of paper. I have never forgotten this wonderful kindness. I hope I was able to express my thanks adequately.

I knew enough English from two years of study to ask questions but not enough to understand the answers. This problem solved itself after a few months, from one day to the next, when suddenly I understood English.

After that one night with the Salvation Army, we boys were moved to a house in the East End of London. Another house within walking distance was found a little later for the girls of the group.

On the 15th March 1939 a group of us were in town to see the tourist sites of London. At Trafalgar Square, the news vendors were shouting,

"Hitler occupies Czechoslovakia."

We hurried to buy a paper. It was a terrible shock, but it was not unexpected - although nobody anticipated Hitler breaking his Munich promises so soon. We were worried about our people back home - yet we could not possibly imagine the depth of the tragedy to come.

ψ

It was about this time that I began to get stomach pains caused by an ulcer. Was it psychosomatic? I do not know. On the whole I was fit and did a lot of sport. I kept doing my work but I always carried a bottle of stomach powder in my pocket.

ψ

I was keen to get down to the real business of training to be a farm worker. Finally after months of waiting, we heard that we could move to the David Eder Farm at Ringlewood, near Maidstone in Kent. There we did *hachshara* with others from the British *Habonim* youth groups, about fifty in all.

The farm, named after a British Zionist, was several hundred acres and run by a Jewish organisation. An English agriculturist was employed to be in charge and train us.

The farm buildings were too small to accommodate us all so we lived in tents while building our own wooden houses. I teamed up with two boys from Germany who had carpentry training and I learnt some of the trade from them.

In September 1939, after Germany invaded Poland, the British government declared war on Germany. Poland was soon defeated and for some months, the situation was quiet. It was the Phoney War when propaganda leaflets were dropped rather than bombs.

We wanted to marry but could not do so legally as our entry permits to Palestine were issued to us as single people: Leah had a certificate and I was expecting an affidavit from the Hebrew University entitling me to a permit. We decided to have a Jewish wedding - it was the real thing to us. (When we eventually married in a registry office in Oxford in November 1940, it seemed a formality.)

The parents of a London girl who was also on *hachshara* kindly invited us to have the wedding in their home and made the necessary arrangements. This was another occasion in our past when I wonder whether we expressed our thanks adequately.

On the day of the wedding, I hitchhiked from Kent - it was raining and my shoes were all muddy. A number of the Farm people came to make up a *minyan*. They travelled in a van, which was used to deliver farm goods to Jewish families in London.

The wedding was held in a Jewish family home with a traditional rabbi in a black coat with a long beard. He agreed to perform the Jewish marriage service without official registration and issued us a *ketuba*, the Jewish marriage contract.

He gave a nice sermon. He appreciated that we were apart from our own families and he gave us some advice for our life together.

"If you get annoyed, count to ten before saying anything. If you get very annoyed, count to a hundred."

I have thought of him every time I have followed this advice. I had a small fee to give to him. I handed him the envelope but he handed it back to Leah.

"Buy yourself a present," he said.

We recall this special day with gratitude, both to the family who gave us the wedding and the admirable rabbi.

✟

After the wedding we went back to the Farm to live - I didn't feel different because our living arrangements were the same - we were still living as a group, like a commune. Soon we made preparations to leave. My gastric problems were getting worse so we moved to London where, I hoped, I would have a better opportunity to obtain treatment.

If we had not left then, we would have had to leave soon. The Farm was on "war territory" near the coast and when the Battle of Britain began, we were considered "aliens" - albeit friendly aliens.

✟

Before I left I received a letter from Max who had escaped to Lithuania. He told me that as soon as the Germans invaded Poland, our parents had insisted that my brothers go east. As for Jacob, I heard from him too, through a note he sent via Switzerland. So both my brothers escaped the Nazis.

Around this time, in 1940, I heard from my mother. She wrote via the Red Cross to say that my father had died. He had a bad heart; in those days there were no by-pass operations and conditions under German occupation were very difficult.

I was shocked to hear of his death but we were in a permanent state of shock.

✟

At first Leah and I lived in the Czech hostel in London run by the Czech Trust Fund, established to give assistance to Czech refugees and funded by a five million pound gift from the British government.

Then we got a bed-sitter. We were getting some financial support from the Czech Trust Fund but we wanted to be as independent as possible. Leah had a job in a clothing factory and treated me to the odd packet of cigarettes.

I got a job sweeping up and generally assisting two building tradesmen who were refurbishing an unoccupied house. I admired their skill - they could wallpaper a room in a couple of hours. One of them showed me how. They thought I did well and requested their employer to give me a raise: after four weeks my wages went up an extra five shillings to twenty-five shillings a week.

But my stomach was still bad and I was admitted into a London hospital. I was not long there when we were told that the hospital was being evacuated to Oxford.

Leah and I had a long term plan to go to Oxford with several groups from different Zionist organisations. It looked as if our plan was being set in motion - although not in the way we had originally intended.

There was no time to contact Leah. But I knew she was re-sourceful and would find me in due course. This was wartime. Everything was in mid-air. We had no choice, no alternatives. Once in Oxford I managed to write to Leah and soon we were reunited.

We were accommodated in a refugee hostel administered by lady volunteers of the Refugee Committee. Leah did some sewing for them to earn some income. One of the volunteers, Mrs. Seaward, employed Leah to convert old dresses into new clothes for her family and herself.

An older lady, a refugee, asked Leah to do some sewing for her but when Leah refused she threatened to inform on her, as she was working without a work permit.

Mrs. Seaward rang her husband. In turn he rang the Home Office and arranged for Leah to have a work permit. There are devils and angels in both camps.

Leah and I each had an Alien Registration Book, like all aliens. If we slept anywhere different, then we had to inform the police who entered the temporary address and the duration of the stay in the book. It was reasonably organised.

At first a Home Office permit was needed for an alien to be employed. This was eased a little later and Labour Exchanges (employment offices) could give jobs to aliens if they could not find a British person to take on the job in the same local authority.

I applied for a job advertised in a newspaper. Cooper and Boffin were looking for a driver for their baker's van.

When Mr. Cooper offered me the job, I asked for a letter to the Labour Exchange so they could give me permission to take the job.

But the man at the Labour Exchange refused to do so. I made my way back to Mr. Cooper to apologise. When I told Mr. Cooper, he rang up the Labour Exchange.

"I have been asking for three months for a driver," he said, "and now I have found one, you say that I cannot have him."

The man at the Labour Exchange said that I could spread bad propaganda when I was delivering the bread. Mr. Cooper offered to transfer me to the wholesale route so I had no contact with the public but the man would not budge. At the same time I could see the funny side of being branded a propagandist.

"If you won't let me have this job, then find me another one," I asked the man at the Labour Exchange.

He offered me a job as kitchen porter at Radley College, a public school, and gave me the required papers to take to the interview. When the College's steward learnt at the interview that I was a medical student, he went to fetch the purser.

"We couldn't possibly put you in the kitchens," the purser exclaimed.

They both hoped that there would be a vacancy in the laboratory as the man in charge of preparing the experiments for the masters was due to be called up. Until then I worked as a college servant looking after three masters. It was a job in the Oxford tradition and

I learnt how to look after a gentleman: to make beds, fold pyjamas, bring a tray of tea and polish shoes. I also had to prepare the trays of food for the boys at meal times and help in the kitchens. A couple of months later I had my own assistant. The money was small but I was fed. Any money honestly earned was better than being a beggar.

According to the Oxford caste system there were three classes of servants and because of my past, I was placed at the top and waited on by a lower grade servant. I was once corrected by a servant because the rules about where to place a knife or when to smoke were precise. I had to improve my table manners a lot to come up to the standard of my classy co-servants. Apart from a few silly mistakes, I learnt my 'trade' quickly.

The Zionist Federation moved their offices to Oxford during the war. In one edition of the *Zionist Review*, an excellent paper which I preferred to the *Jewish Chronicle*, the editorial urged every Zionist to give one week's wages to a Joint Palestinian Appeal. I added my board and lodgings to my servant's wages and took this to the Zionist Federation office. The man in charge looked aghast. He was not expecting anyone to take him seriously. Or perhaps he was thinking of Rabbi Hillel who said that charity should always be given anonymously!

Although I had my room at the college, I was able to leave for Oxford to join Leah in the hostel a few times a week. There were a number of continental doctors in Oxford who were not permitted to practise at the beginning of the war. The university would put some rooms at their disposal where interesting speakers were invited to lecture them. I was accepted into that group and attended some of the lectures. On one occasion Dr. Chain, who worked with Professor Florey on the development of penicillin, gave us a lecture on this project.

❧

One of my Masters at Radley College was Dr. Clayton, head of the maths department. He encouraged me to use his library and even tried unsuccessfully to get me a job in a research laboratory in Oxford. He had a good sense of humour. I once walked in with his tray of tea when he was tutoring a student.

"If you have any problems with your work, ask him," he said pointing at me.

The man I was to replace in the laboratory was not called up and I decided to apply for a course of training for war work. While waiting to be called to a training centre, I worked at Cooper and Boffin as a night-shift baker on twelve-hour shifts. It was gruelling work and with my bad stomach, I had to give up this job.

❧

Fortunately I was called to the Government Training Centre in Slough. I originally applied to be trained as engineering draughtsman but had to take a course as an engineering machinist. At that time foreigners were not considered safe with drawings of war equipment but having gone through one third of my machinist training, I learnt from another 'friendly alien' that we were now permitted to do the draughtsmanship course.

I requested an interview with the Training Centre manager who accepted me as a trainee draughtsman but warned that I would have to pass tests in Logarithms and Trigonometry. To his surprise, I found the tests easy. The six-month course was interesting. There were fifteen of us, most of them well educated people who had left their peace time jobs to train for war work. We all passed three exams and were sent to factories needing draughtsmen.

❧

Around this time I had a Red Cross letter from my mother.*
On one side the message was typed for official purposes. On the

* See PLATE 11

back was the original hand-written message.

She wrote, "I am happy about the news, that (Mother's brothers) are healthy. Don't worry about me, I am tough. The lack of knowledge about Max and Joseph is worrying me. Perhaps Uncle Simon has some news. Take care."

⚘

After my training, we returned to Oxford - it felt like our hometown at that time. My work was at Witney, just outside Oxford. About two months later, our first child was due to be born.

When the labour contractions began late at night, I called the St. John's Ambulance - then a voluntary service. The driver took us both to the hospital two miles away.

"How are you going to get back?" he asked me.

"I suppose I'll walk," I said.

"I'll take you home," he said.

He drove back to the ambulance station, took his car and drove me home -even though it was right out of his way. I was very impressed because he would not use the ambulance service unofficially and went to such trouble to get me home in his private car.

⚘

After Michael was born, I had to see to it that he was circumcised. Our friends the Schmidts (or Smiths as they became known), were in charge of a hostel for Jewish boys and active in the Jewish community. They arranged for a *mohel* to come to the hospital and perform the circumcision. Samuel Smith, or Mulo as we called him, was a *Cohen* so he held the baby during the ceremony. I was the happy father when the operation was concluded. There was no *minyan,* or celebration, as this was a most depressing time of the war.

If I can jump ahead, many years later, after eighteen years in Australia and the Smith's years in Israel, it was Mulo Smith who again held our grandsons, Jonathan and Richard, children of Judy and Robin, at their circumcisions.

♦

My first job was in Witney, ten miles from Oxford, with Integral Auxiliary Equipment Ltd. It was a shadow factory of a London engineering company set up in the building of a blanket manufacturer. Shadow factories were required in case the original factories were bombed.

We manufactured high-pressure gear pumps used in the hydraulic systems of warplanes. At first I designed equipment needed in the manufacture of components for the pumps, but soon was also busy planning the production methods and work schedules. We had a second shadow factory in Birmingham where I spent a few days a week for some months.

My university education in physics and medicine really helped. Now I believe that it doesn't matter what you study because it teaches you how to learn.

♦

In 1944, after two years, I had a disagreement with my superior. He wanted me to request items even though we had enough capacity in that type. I did not give way and this, coupled with my bad stomach, made me decide to quit. In retrospect it seems rather reckless. I had no other job lined up, a wife and small son to support and I had to give up the accommodation that went with the job. At the time we were young and for some reason, I was not worried. Leah was always a strong support, a gutsy girl. But what were my worries compared to those of my people?

♦

The end of the war was in the air. In 1944, I attended night classes at the Cardiff Technical College in sanitary engineering, which together with my medical studies would prepare me for work with an organisation that was to take care of European Jewish survivors. Sadly, I abandoned the idea as my health was not up to it.

We knew things were bad in Europe - we heard rumours - but

we did not know how bad. It was only after the war that we heard of the systematic efficiency used to murder the Jews.

I soon found a job in South Wales as a jig and tool draughtsman in an aircraft body factory called Helliwells. My employer was only obliged to find accommodation for me, so at first Leah and Michael stayed behind in Witney.

When I reported for my first morning at work, suitcase in hand, no digs had yet been found for me. The young woman in the personnel department tried all day but, by the evening when I returned to her office, had found nothing. Rather than letting me down, she telephoned her mother, Mrs John who offered me temporary accommodation. I was embarrassed to accept but I had no choice. There was helpfulness during the war but the Johns were altogether special and we became life-long friends.

"I will only charge you exactly what you cost me," said Daisy John when I got to their house.

"We have two sons about your age in the Forces away from home," Oliver John said later when we were chatting. "We hope that if they were in a similar position, someone else would do the same for them."

Some weeks after my move to Cardiff, thanks to the Johns, Leah and Michael were able to join me. A widowed cousin of theirs lived alone in a semi-detached house and they persuaded her to share it with me.

Both the Johns were active chapel people and Daisy had a wonderful voice. Their daughter, Aerona Newton John, was a teacher doing war work. During our stay in Cardiff, Oliver had a bad heart attack. I was the only one he wanted to visit him in hospital.

When Judy was born in 1946, the Johns wanted to lend us a christening robe so that we could have her christened. They were not trying to convert us - they just did not know the differences between our religions.

Our last contact with the family was in Australia with their older son, Bryn Newton John, after Oliver and Daisy John had passed away. Bryn was a university lecturer in Australia and the father of Olivia Newton-John, the famous singer and actress, although we never met her.

Refugees have a difficult life and reason to complain. However, some of the help and friendship we received outweighed all our problems.

⁂

My work in the aircraft body factory was quite successful and I soon became an unofficial assistant to the chief draughtsman. The war was coming to an end and I could not see my future with the company specialising in fighter aircraft and, after a year's employment, I left in April 1945.

Again I had no job to go to. Looking back, it seems very irresponsible and Leah did not discourage me but somehow it worked out.

I was on the bus going to work and I said to a fellow engineer and Jew,

"I won't be travelling with you next week – I gave in my notice this week."

"What will you do?" he asked with concern.

Also on the bus was Mr. Fränkel, one of the directors of Aero Zip Fasteners, and someone I knew from local Zionists meetings. Suddenly my friend leaned across the aisle and said to him,

"Don't you have a job for Weber?"

I felt so embarrassed.

"Well, why don't you see the Works Manager?" Mr. Fränkel replied.

The Works Manager put me on six weeks probation. He probably felt obliged because he may have thought I was some kind of protégé of Mr. Fränkel. I did not want pity just because I was a fellow Jew from the continent and I nearly did not take up the offer. But Leah encouraged me,

"Why not give it a try?" she said.

Within a few weeks I was reassured that I was part of the team – and on my own merits. One day I mentioned to a manager that I was on probation. He looked shocked and said:

"Good God, you must realise that you are one of us?"

I stayed with Aero for the next 31 years.

The end of the war in Europe came as great relief and the next thing to await was the end of the war in the Pacific. Now that the war in Europe was over I could have the operation for my stomach ulcers. I was lying in hospital in August 1945 listening to the radio when I heard that an atom bomb had been dropped on Hiroshima. I was very shocked and very sad. I had never heard of such a powerful weapon that could wipe out twenty thousand people in one blast. More were to die from the after-effects of radiation. It was terrible but it brought the war with Japan to an end.

PART IV - The Fate of the Ost Family - Leah

I n 1940 my mother wrote via the Red Cross to say that my father was suffering from Parkinson's disease. In 1942 my parents were taken to Theresienstadt and, shortly afterwards my mother wrote to say that he had died. He had been very ill and was unable to get medical treatment.

After the war I was convinced that I would hear from my mother. I went every week to the Red Cross and tried every channel but I heard nothing. If she was alive she would have written. Gradually I began to accept that she could not have survived but at the same time I could not help hoping that I would hear from her again.

I did not hear what had happened to my mother until 1948, on my first visit to Israel. I met one of my mother's cousins who had survived Auschwitz. She came over to my brother Salo's and told me what she knew.

"I was in Theresienstadt with your mother. She was working in the hospital as a nurse. A year after your father died, all the doctors and nurses were ordered to Auschwitz. Before she left, your mother gave me a tin of sardines she had hidden."

Hilde told me that the transport of doctors and nurses from Theresienstadt was sent straight to the gas chambers on arrival at Auschwitz. The year would have been 1945. It was terrible to hear.

Shortly after arriving in England, I had received a letter from

Erna Fränkel. She was living in our family apartment with her husband Oskar.

"We would like to come to England - can you help?" she wrote.

We did not know which way to turn. We went to Woburn House to make enquiries. We tried as hard as we could but there seemed to be no way to get permission for her to enter Britain. Strangely enough, by chance I saw Stana in the street but I did not stop to talk to him. I just swore under my breath because Erna was trapped in Czechoslovakia. The tragedy is that if Erna had been allowed to marry him, she might have escaped to England and still be alive.

We continued to write. When Sigo and I got married, Erna made me a wedding dress which I never saw because, as I mentioned earlier, when the wedding crate finally turned up in 1939, it was empty. The last time I heard of Erna was in a letter from my mother sent via the Red Cross in 1942.*

When the war ended I still hoped that I would hear from Erna that she was hidden somewhere. I wrote to the Red Cross and the refugee committees. I tried every channel but there was not a sound. It was as if she had disappeared. Since the war I have approached every agency I can think of to find some record of her death but I have never found anything.

On the Kibbutz Givat Chayim, there is a memorial with the names of the Jews killed in Czechoslovakia. Hilde found the names of our parents but she did not find Erna's name. Whenever I went back to Prague, I always inquired after Erna. No one has ever been able to tell me what happened. In one synagogue there is a record of the Czech Jews killed in camps. My parents, aunts and uncles are recorded there - but not Erna.

I often wonder how she died. The thought of my lovely vivacious sister dying a violent death is very hard to bear.

* See PLATE 12

My brother Salo, sailed to Palestine illegally from Romania in the winter of 1939. The British forces would not let the ship dock. For four months the ship stayed on the water and half the people on board died of dysentery and hunger. My brother became deaf in one ear from this ordeal.

The *Hagana* in Haifa smuggled him off board and into Palestine. He and his fellow survivors took assumed names and lost themselves. As soon as he arrived he wrote to me at the farm in England in 1939, so I knew then that he was safe.

Salo arrived in Palestine with nothing - we sent him what we could. Sigo even sent him one of his suits. When he first landed in Palestine, Salo stayed with Hilde on her *kibbutz* and worked very hard in the fields.

I saw him again in Israel on my first visit. At home he used to entertain a roomful of people with jokes but, after the trauma of the boat journey, he was never the same again. In some part of his heart, he was a broken man. Salo did not have a profession. He worked as a driver for a fizzy drinks company delivering to shops. He liked to be busy and made a good living. When I visited, we talked about our parents. He was a good fellow - I really liked him. Salo died in 1982. His wife, also called Leah, died a few years ago.

Salo(Shlomo) and Leah had three children - two daughters and a son - Batel, Esther and Yehudah. Esther has two children, Enat and Idor. Batel's son was born on the same day that her father, my brother Salo, died. Yehudah's marriage broke up and he has not stayed in touch with his family. We do not know if he has any children.

When I left Hilde Fanta at Prague station, I expected to see her soon in Palestine. Hilde went with her group to a *kibbutz*. They were supposed to go to school but there was no money for their education. Every day a teacher came and they learned Hebrew.

All through the war I received letters from Hilde and Salo. We always sent them parcels - whatever we could afford.

The next time I saw her was after the war - and it was as if we had never been parted. We spoke as if we had seen each other the day before. The only difference was in our lifestyles. When I first visited them, they lived in one room in a wooden hut on a *kibbutz*. When it was time for bed, they pulled another bed from under theirs and we all shared one room.

Life has been hard for Hilde. She was torn away from her family and her studies at the age of fourteen. Her natural development was arrested and this can affect a person's confidence. She married Hans Fanta whom she met on *Youth Aliyah*. In Israel he was known as Ze'ev and he was a very nice fellow. Hilde ran a café and Ze'ev worked as a mechanic. As refugees, they had been robbed of their education and were only trained for physical work. Ze'ev died three years ago and Hilde lives in an old people's home in Kfar Sava which she likes because she has company there.

Hilde and Ze'ev had two children - Dalia who is a kitchen and bathroom designer and Gadi Pen who is now an engineer. He took early retirement from the Israeli Air Force where he was a colonel. When he was with the military, his name was changed to Pen for security reasons. I remember him visiting us in the seventies in London - although he was on official duties, he always dressed in jeans and T-shirt when he was travelling. He could not afford to advertise that he was a high-ranking Israeli military official - it would have put his life in danger.

Y

The last time I saw my aunt Tante Helena Rosen was before the war in Ostrava, just before she left for Palestine. Her children were my Zionist cousins and her son Shlomo was a leading figure in the *Chalutzik* movement. It was thanks to him that she and her husband left Czechoslovakia in 1935.

The next time I saw her was on my first visit to Israel. I was staying with Salo in his flat in Tel Aviv and on my first morning, when I was still asleep, there was a ring at the doorbell. It was my Tante Helena with an enormous bunch of flowers. She could not wait to see me, her sister's daughter. She burst into tears.

"Why couldn't my sister be here?" she said.

She was very unhappy; she missed her family deeply. The sisters and brothers of my mother's family had been so close. She was the eldest and it was terrible for her to survive her younger siblings. Her husband, a Hebrew scholar, missed his family too and not long after my visit he died of a broken heart.

Tante Helena died of old age on Kibbutz Givat Chayim where her daughter lived. Tante Helena had eight children. Two had died before the war and the remaining six were with her in Israel. Shlomo Rosen, always a leading light, became Minister of Immigration for Israel. Now only three are left: Avi, Channan and Wili.

During the 1950s I went nearly every year to Israel. Even after we moved to Australia, I would visit every two years or so. I went mainly to see my relatives: my sister Hilde, my brother Salo, Tante Helena and my six cousins.

✡

In this photograph* you see my maternal grandmother, Fani Schlachet, surrounded by her seven grown up children. She had five daughters and two sons. Their spouses are also pictured. My grandmother is at the centre of the seated ladies - third from the left. She died of natural causes before the war. Five of her seven children perished in the Holocaust.

From left to right at the back, there is my mother's sister Tante Anna and her husband Eugene. They and their daughter Lotte perished in the camps and their names are recorded in Prague and Givat Chayim.

* See PLATE 1

Next is my father Moshe and my mother Teresa. As we know, he died in Theresienstadt of illness and my mother died in the gas chambers of Auschwitz. Next is Onkel Hutterer (he was known by his surname). An uncle by marriage, he was the husband of Tante Ida (who is seated in the front row). They had two sons both of whom died during the war. One was a medical student who was shot by the Germans when he was a soldier with the Czech Army. Ida and her husband were taken to Auschwitz. The younger son was shot in front of his mother when he tried to stop her being interned. Some cousins who were eye-witnesses told me.

Tante Helena's husband, Onkel Samuel, is next. My mother's eldest sister Tante Helena and Onkel Samuel escaped to Palestine before the war thanks to their pioneering Zionist children, who all survived.

Next is Onkel Heinrich, one of my mother's two brothers. He was married to Tante Regina who is pictured next to him. He died before the war and Tante Regina went to Vienna. His son from his first marriage escaped to Romania when war broke out but I do not know what happened to him or his mother Tante Regina.

Next is Onkel William (Wili), my mother's other brother. He was married to Tante Gusti (short for Augusti) who is seated in the front row. They had two daughters Herta and Doris. During the war Onkel Wili and his daughter walked to Russia. Herta survived but Willi died of starvation. Tante Gusti and their other daughter Doris dyed their hair blonde and spent the war disguised as non-Jews working as a cook and maid in the home of a German aristocrat. After the war Tante Gusti and her two daughters, Herta and Doris,* settled in Australia. I met up with my aunt and cousins when we were there and we became close to them and their children. Tante Gusti died in Australia but my children are still in contact with her grandchildren, Caroline and Steven (from Doris) and Peter and Evelyn (from Herta).

* See PLATE 9

Next is Onkel Heinrich. He was a Schlachet cousin and he married my mother's sister Tante Marie (seated in the front row). They had five children. The youngest died with them in Auschwitz but the others escaped to Palestine before the war and one, Hella, is still alive. On the front row, seated from left to right are my mother's sister Tante Ida, my mother's sister Tante Helena, my mother's mother (my grandmother) Fani, my mother's sister-in-law Tante Gusti (Augustina) and my mother's sister Tante Marie.

My father, Moshe Ost, had a sister and a brother as well as a half-brother. Here is what I know about them. His sister, Rosa (Ost) Steiner, lived in Krakow in Poland where her husband Bernard had the city's first steam bakery in the twenties. My mother would visit for holidays, although I never went. I was told as a child that Tante Rosa's little girl looked like my identical twin! Tante Rosa and her family disappeared and we never heard what happened to them during the war. My uncle Hermann said that they all perished in camps in Poland.

My father's brother, Leonis Ost, went to America before the war and settled in Brooklyn where he had a factory for ladies' underwear. He married and would frequently write to his brother, my father.

My father's mother had remarried her late husband's brother and they had a son, Hermann Ost. Hermann had a private Jewish bank in Rozvadov in Poland where my father's family came from.

Hermann's two children were distinguished - his daughter became a doctor and his son a violinist. Hermann's wife was a concert flautist, well known in Poland.

During the war, Hermann went into hiding with his family in the woods of Russia. After the war the family emigrated to Israel. Hermann's son, Romek Ost the violinist, played in the Israeli Opera and now teaches music in schools. His sister Sara is a doctor in an old people's home in Tel Aviv.

PART IV - The Fate of the Weber Family - Sigo

My father Arnold Weber died in Teschen in 1940 from heart failure. I heard this news from my mother who wrote via the Red Cross. I knew that my father had died during the war because my mother had written to tell me. But what of my mother? As soon as the war was over, I tried to find out if she was alive. As I did not hear from her and she had our address, I had to assume the worst.

Then came the confirmation. My brothers, with whom I was in touch after the war, discovered that my mother had died in Auschwitz in 1943. She was there at the same time as the daughters of Uncle Sigmund and they saw her "go to the shower," as they called it.

After the war Max heard from one of our Christian tenants who had managed to visit my mother when she was in Auschwitz and smuggle food through the fence. My mother knew she was going to die and she wanted her children to inherit something. My mother gave her a pair of shoes with jewellery concealed in one of the heels. Our neighbour gave these shoes to Max after the war. The jewellery was shared between the wives of the three brothers and Leah received diamond earrings. We still have them - they have new mountings and one of the stones has been replaced.

As a boy, I was close to the children of my mother's two brothers, Sigmund and Joseph Farber. Both families lived on the Polish side of the border, a short train ride away. I used to stay with my cousins during the summer holidays - it was my uncle Sigmund who taught me to play chess. My uncles and their wives died in Auschwitz.

Uncle Sigmund had three daughters and a son. Leo, the youngest, died of pneumonia in Russia during the war. The three daughters Bertha, Ida and Gretka, and Bertha's husband and their two children were sent to Auschwitz where they were strong enough to do forced labour. They survived thanks to their foreman. He was in charge of the forced labour shop in which they worked. He covered up for any of them if they were too sick to work - otherwise it would have been the end of them. Now and then the three daughters sent a piece of jewellery to his wife to say thank you.

After liberation, the three daughters wrote a statement, at the foreman's request, saying that he had treated them as well as he could. This was to help him should he be questioned.

After the war Sigmund's three daughters, with Bertha's husband Freddie Leimsieder and their two daughters, who also survived Auschwitz, returned to their home in Poland.

There were pogroms in Poland and they all went by boat to Israel. Gretka had married after the camps but was widowed by the time she left for Israel. Ida's husband did not survive the war and she did not remarry.

When Leah went on her first visit to Israel after the war, Ze'ev (her sister Hilde's husband) took her in his van to look for my cousins. After scouring three different refugee camps, Leah found them living in a Ma'abara "tent city" in Haifa. She stayed the night in the camp and had noodles and sugar cooked on a little Primus stove.

"Whatever you do, buy Gretka a sewing machine," I had told Leah before she left for Israel.

Leah did exactly that and Gretka then had a tool to earn her living as Leah had done.

Joseph Farber, my mother's brother and his wife, died in a camp during the war. He had six children. Only three survived the Holocaust, Nettie, Salo and Jakub. They escaped to the Soviet Union when the Germans invaded Poland. Salo joined the Polish army in Russia and came with the army, via the Middle East, to the UK. Salo married in London and later joined his sister in the U.S.A. After he died, I lost touch with his wife and two sons.

Nettie and her husband emigrated to the U.S.A. after the war and had two daughters. Nettie passed away a few years ago and I lost touch with her family. Jakub, the youngest, married a Russian woman and stayed in Russia. He too has passed away.

Onkel Simon was a much older brother of my mother who left Poland before the end of the century. My mother had an "older generation" of siblings whom I never met because we moved away from her hometown in 1921.

Onkel Simon lived in Buffalo, U.S.A. I first visited him in 1948 when I was in the States on a business trip. Simon spoke seven languages fluently and knew the Bible and Torah inside out. He believed in communist ideas and was, what I would call, a fundamentalist atheist. He had seventeen children of whom fourteen survived. The great majority can be found in *Who's Who*, including his daughter Gertrude Helene Schwartz, one of the first female lawyers, Professor Sydney Farber, a pioneer in chemotherapy, Professor Marvin Farber, Emeritus Professor of Philosophy and Eugene Farber, a world renowned dermatologist.

I was not as close to my father's brothers, Rudolph and Bernard Weber. My father's sister was widowed and remarried my mother's youngest brother, Sigmund - the uncle who taught me chess. Both Uncle Rudolph and Bernard died before the war. As for my uncles' children, I only heard of two survivors, Artur Weber, his wife and one of his sisters. There may have been other relatives who survived but I have not heard from or of them and I assume that they were killed during the war.

✣

During the war my brother Max went to Lithuania ahead of the advancing German Army and was able to write to us from there. He had a job and was hoping to return to Czechoslovakia and save my parents. But when he refused to enrol in the Russian Army, he was sent to a punitive camp in Siberia. I never heard from him during his time in the gulag.

✣

After the invasion of the Soviet Union by the Germans, the Soviets had formed a Czech army unit as part of their own forces. The army numbered several thousand and about half were Jewish.

I later found out that Max had been given the opportunity to volunteer for the Czech army unit and was freed. This saved Max's life because many died from malnutrition in the notorious gulag.

The next time I had news of him was when I read about him during the war in a Czech newspaper. The paper, printed in Britain, had an article with a photograph of the award-giving ceremony after the battle of Sokolov. My brother, an officer in the Czech Army, was mentioned for his brave actions in the rear-guard holding back the advancing Germans and was awarded a medal.

Max was an Adjutant to General Svoboda who later became President of Communist Czechoslovakia. Before the war Max had been in the Czech Army for eighteen months compulsory service, so he quickly progressed up the ranks. By the time he left the army after the war, he was a colonel

✣

When Germany invaded Poland, my parents urged both of my brothers to flee east. My eldest brother Jacob went to the Urals. Like Max, he signed up for the newly formed Czech Army in Russia, probably in 1942, and that is how he and Max met up again. Like Max, he soon gained officer rank. Once after a battle, Jacob was wounded and would have been abandoned by the army had his brother Max not gone back to rescue him. Both he and Max were wounded twice and gained many distinctions. Both brothers were demobilised after the war and settled in Prague.

In 1946 when Judy was just six weeks old, Max visited us in Cardiff in his Czech army uniform. It was the first time that Leah had met him. He was only given permission for a three-day stay in Britain - on the fourth day the police arrived at our house to see if he had left. It seemed a strange way to treat an allied army hero with a chestful of medals.

I went to see Max and Jacob in Prague in 1947. The city had suffered little damage from the war and it was wonderful to be re-united with my brothers. Max and Jacob had shops next door to each other. As war heroes, they both had good business contacts in a land of post-war scarcity. Jacob sold shoes and Max had a drapery.

General Svoboda offered Max a post as military attaché in either Moscow or Warsaw. Max replied that, had the post been in London, he would have taken it but that he did not want to live in a communist country.

In 1948, when the communists gained the upper hand in the Czech government, I made a special trip to Prague to tell my brothers to get out while they could. The plan was that the three of us with our families would settle in Israel and go into the manufacture of zip fasteners.

In 1949, Max went with the Jewish army brigade formed in Czechoslovakia to join Israel in the fight against its enemies. Max took a major part in organising this brigade. When they arrived in Israel, there was an armistice and Israel was not prepared to incor-porate the brigade as a unit. Each member could join the army as an individual and as soon as the officers could speak Hebrew, they would receive their original rank.

Max took it hard. He felt promises made had not been kept. His non-Jewish wife, Marta, was pregnant and wanted to return to Prague. Max followed soon after. Jacob - or Kuba as we called him - his wife Sala and their two-year-old Yirka, were all set to go to Israel; a container had already been sent ahead with their goods. But Max said, "Don't come," and they stayed in Prague.

I was very disappointed. This was the end of a dream of the three brothers working and living in Israel.

Jacob became ill with pancreatitis. Perhaps if he had been in Israel he could have been saved because Max always felt that the medical treatment he received in Prague was not good enough. Kuba was the best of us with his lovely singing voice and a great sense of humour - a very decent man. He died in his thirties, a young man.

Max worked as a systems analyst. He had a passport as he frequently had to travel to Vienna. After the Russians invaded Czechoslovakia in 1968, it was time to get out. They sedated the cat and put her in an overnight bag. As they left their apartment, the building's concierge - whose job was to be the eyes and ears of the Secret Service - asked Marta where they were going.

"I'm just taking Max to the station," she said. "He is going to Vienna again."

"I'll come too," said the concierge.

At the station, Marta took her to a restaurant for a drink.

"I'll be back in a minute," Marta said but instead she hopped on a train with Max. They continued their journey to Switzerland where they had friends. Their daughter, Sylva, who was in Germany, joined them there later.

✢

Leah and I were about to travel to Europe and the U.S.A. around that time and a visit to Max in Prague was included in the itinerary. Just before we left Sydney, I had a feeling that something might

happen and I sent Max the addresses of Michael in New York and
the head of Aero Zip Fasteners in the U.K. On arrival in the U.K.
two telegrams in Czech awaited me, one from Max in Switzerland
and one copied faithfully by Michael who had heard from Max but
did not understand the message in Czech.

Max and Marta liked Switzerland. They both found employment and stayed. Sylva married Bruno Nägele and they have two
sons, Philip and Martin. We kept in touch over the years, with visits
and telephone calls every couple of weeks.

Early in 1995, Sylva telephoned me. She felt that they had not
sufficiently celebrated her father's eightieth birthday two years
earlier and she invited us to Basle to celebrate a double birthday for
the two brothers, my eightieth and Max's eighty-second. Sadly Max
passed away and our visit, instead of being one of celebration, was
one of great sadness.

PART V - The Next 50 Years

Sigo:

When Leah was expecting Judy I went to an auction and made a bid on a house. I had just managed to scrape together the ten per cent of the sum required. The Managing Director had promised to help me with housing and he agreed that Aero buy the house. So we lived in a company house all the time we were in Cardiff and even the telephone bill was paid for by Aero (I paid for electricity). The moment when Aero bought the house was one of those key moments when I felt I was on my way up.

Judy was born on 6th February 1946. The same nurse who looked after me when I had my stomach operation was there on the maternity ward.

"She's a miniature Mr. Weber," she exclaimed.

Indeed Judy possesses a certain type of intelligence inherited from my mother who was a bright woman. Judy was born at a difficult time although we did not realise it at the time – we were coming to terms with the end of the war and the loss of our mothers. But look, the birth of a baby is always a wonderful thing.

Although I was doing well at work, we did not feel settled. Palestine was still on our minds. We were still asking ourselves, "What shall we do? Where shall we live?"

The war had made it impossible for us to go to Palestine but we remained faithful to the idea of a Jewish state and our part in it as members of the *Hechalutz*, the Zionist pioneer movement. We were active Zionists and helped collect funds for Zionist causes. The thought of living in a commune no longer appealed to us as we became a family but going to live in Palestine was still an option. So much so that I asked for our flight to Palestine to be written into my contract with Aero. Also, I asked for a three-year contract rather than a five-year-one.

In 1947 I received a telephone call from *Hechaluz* in London. "Can you make yourself available immediately?" said one of the organisers. I and the family were asked to join the illegal *aliyah* (*Aliyah Bet*). Legal immigration (*Aliyah Aleph*) to the future Jewish homeland in Palestine was strictly limited by Great Britain.

We would have had to travel to France, ostensibly on holiday. We would board an *aliyah* ship, which was expected to be arrested by the British Navy and the people taken to a camp for illegal immigrants in Cyprus. There my real work would begin, training concentration camp survivors for life in Palestine.

It was a painfully difficult decision but the welfare of our children, Michael then five and Judy then one, had to come first.

The declaration of the Jewish state in 1948 was a very great event for Leah and me. Every Jew was entitled to enter and become a citizen. Had it existed before the war, how many Jewish lives could have been saved?

To us and others, the creation of Israel was not the end of the Zionist effort. The young state had to be defended and built up in a hurry to receive hundreds of thousands of Jews from all over the world. Israel was never out of our minds.

Leah:

Like Sigo, I wondered if we would emigrate to the new state of Israel. But the older the children became, the harder it would have been to uproot. Gradually the dream faded although I visited Israel every year or two.

I love Israel. Even if I disagree with the Israelis, I still feel at home there. It is amazing to have witnessed its transformation from an under-developed country to a developed one.

When Sigo had to go into hospital again because of his stomach ulcer, I stood by his bedside and he looked so terrible that I fainted. That's when I knew I was pregnant.

We were thrilled. We hoped for a girl and a girl it was. "She looks exactly like my mother," said Sigo, when he first saw Judy. Even today he calls her Malka. Judy was such a sweet baby, very friendly and always smiling. She and Michael were great friends except when he teased her! They are good friends to this day.

Sigo flew to Prague in 1947 to be reunited with his two brothers for the first time. During this time Michael became so ill with peritonitis after a burst appendix that I had to call Sigo to come home.

It was touch and go for Michael whether he would survive. But thankfully he got better and he had his fifth birthday in hospital.

His birthday wish was to have a suit like Daddy's with an inside pocket in the jacket. Luckily the same nurse who was there at Judy's birth and Sigo's stomach operation, was on Michael's ward and she - against the very strict rules of the time – allowed us at least to show Michael the present we had bought him. The only sadness was that he could not try it on in hospital. But when he recovered and was at home, he wore it for Sunday best and was very proud of it.

⚜

We moved to Whitchurch in Cardiff to our first new house bought by Aero for us to live in. One day a woman about my age came to call. "You've just moved in, haven't you?" she said. Her face was friendly.

Audrey Welsh was my neighbour. She lived in the house opposite with her husband, a bank manager, and their small child, Elizabeth, who was about Michael's age. We hit it off immediately and did everything together.

Audrey and I would go to London once a month on the breakfast train. We would shop in the mornings, have a snack lunch and catch a matinée in the West End before going home. Her family were devout Catholics. She would invite us for Boxing Day lunch and I would invite her to Seder night. Once at her house there was a young priest who tried to talk me into converting - I just laughed. I thought the idea was very funny.

Next door to Audrey was the Chief of Mounties in Canada, then still a commonwealth country. The wife was so excited when they were invited to Buckingham Palace.

"I need a hat and new gloves when presented at court," she would say if you bumped into her. Audrey and I killed ourselves laughing.

When we moved to Australia in 1955, Audrey wrote. "Tell me what you need and I'll send it." I have very happy memories of Audrey and her family. I had a good time in Cardiff. We had good friends and they make all the difference.

A week after Michael's *barmitzvah*, when he was thirteen and Judy was nine, we moved to Australia. Once there we joined a Jewish community. Although we are not observant, we always identified with Jewish people. I am trusting but I always feel particularly safe in Jewish company. There is an understanding there.

Now I knew that we were not going to live in Israel, my interest in Zionism broadened out to other, mainly Jewish - organisations. I was involved with Wizo activities and I became president of the Women's Lodge of B'nai B'rith for several years. Twice a year I would throw open our big house in Lindfield, a suburb of Sydney, for charity appeal functions. It was a lot of work but it felt worthwhile. Together with Sigo we would make a collection for the Jewish National Fund. It was important for both of us to play an active role and do what we could.

In 1958 we both joined B'nai B'rith, the oldest Jewish service organisation in the world. In 1961 Sigo was president of Albert Einstein Lodge (B'nai B'rith) and in 1964 I became president. Sigo was also active in other organisations including the Leo Baeck Lodge, United Israel Appeal, the Zionist Federation and Kayemet l'Israel (KKL). He was also a leading figure in the Rotary Club in Australia. Amazingly he also found time to play tennis and golf.

Sigo:

In 1955, I was sent by Aero Zip Fasteners to Australia, on a fact-finding mission. Should we open a company there? I was only a Chief Engineer and by all rights, a director should have made this decision. But I was considered bright and my opinion was respected. I made a thorough investigation and conducted many interviews, talking to all and sundry. Finally I dictated an eight-page report from my hotel.

"It will be difficult but I suggest that we go ahead right away – we have already waited long enough," was my conclusion.

The managing director cabled me back,

"Go ahead."

So I bought a building and extra land in Australia and three months later I travelled by boat with all the equipment needed to set up a factory.

Thus I helped establish Aero's first subsidiary in Australia – only we were not allowed to use the word 'zip' so it was called Aero Slide Fasteners. This company did very well and when Aero was sold off to a US conglomerate, the most profitable company was the one in Australia.

From 1973 to 1975 I was managing director of Aero Zip Fasteners. I never made up my mind to make it to the top. I never schemed or climbed over others to get there. My motivation was that whatever job I did, I did it right. If there was a problem I'd pace my office up and down, thinking, "There must be a way."

I worked on the principle that a deal is only good if it is good for both parties. For it is better if nobody is the loser.

Leah:

When we were in Australia, I became ill with cancer and had a serious operation. My doctor said:

"Nothing can happen to you - you are a survivor."

I was shocked - I had never seen myself in these terms. But when I look back I am astonished how much I have had to take. Somehow I have managed to take it all in my stride. I was brought up not to make a fuss and it's amazing what you get used to - when you have no choice!

ᐁ

Michael attended Sydney Grammar School and Judy attended North Sydney High. Michael went on to study medicine at Sydney University.

When he was trying to decide what to study, he said,

"I suppose Dad would like me to do medicine - I will finish what he didn't."

Judy read computer studies at Sydney University and then became a computer programmer.

Michael went on to study post-graduate medicine in America where he met his future wife Sandra. In 1971 we went to their wedding in New York. Michael had a post in a Sydney hospital and he and Sandra were still in Australia when we returned to Britain.

ᐁ

Judy came back with us to London when we moved. At first we rented a flat in St. John's Wood and then we moved to our flat in Kelso Place where we have been for the last twenty-six years.

At first I was homesick and missed my friends back in Australia but I still had old friends in London and gradually I stopped missing life in Sydney.

Judy and Robin were married on the 29th August 1975.

PART VI - Reflections
Auschwitz 1995

Leah:

We never wanted to live in Czechoslovakia again. We would say: "We are not going back," when we were in Oxford during the war. People would exclaim: "But you speak proper Czech!" - for most Czech refugees only spoke German.

"I hate them," I answered.

I liked visiting Prague, it is fascinating city. I can still speak the language but I feel like a foreigner.

But in 1995, for the first time in sixty or so years, we visited my home-town. I had not visited Ostrava before because it was too painful. The trip was planned with Sigo and some friends - we hired a car and travelled through Czechoslovakia. We also intended to visit Auschwitz, for the first time.

I was shocked when I saw the city of my youth. It was empty of everything I remembered. All the parks I used to play in or the big coffee houses where Jews sat in the afternoon - everything looked so shabby, down-at-heel and neglected. The German theatre no longer existed and, although there was still a Czech theatre, the programme was not very exciting.

We went to a *Rosh Hashana* service in a flat converted to a Jewish centre. It was a short service with about thirty congregants. I found out afterwards that not one person there had been born in Ostrava. There was no one there who had any connection with my family.

family.

I felt like a stranger. This was a place which used to be full of people I knew. The memories came flooding back. On every corner I imagined seeing my aunts and uncles, my cousins, their friends and relatives. But a place without people is nothing.

I visited our old apartment and stood outside on the pavement. I did not want to go in - I felt no connection. My grandmother had lived a ten minute walk away and Sigo and I went to look at her old house and the shop were I used to do her shopping. But nothing was as I remembered it.

The cultured, lively and extrovert Jews were missing. Ostrava was no longer Little Paris but a dowdy little mining town.

I am glad I saw Ostrava but it was so distressing to see how it had changed that I made up my mind never to return.

From Ostrava we travelled by train to Krakow in Poland. I would have liked to have seen where Tante Rosa, my father's sister, had lived, but I thought, "What's the point of looking at a house?"

From Krakow we travelled to Auschwitz. I did not want to go but Sigo encouraged me. We had a very good guide who was in-formed and gave us the facts in a clear way. We had seen many films but it was much more clean and tidy than we imagined. This seemed to make it all the more gruesome. I was devastated. It was a terrible experience to see the place where so many people were taken to be killed. I was glad to leave. For a few days afterwards I could hardly speak.

The Holocaust has shaped my life. It got more and more horri-ble after the war when you heard details from talking to survivors. You get very selfish and you wanted to know what happened to your people. There was no other conversation - even today when we meet up with friends, the conversation comes back to the Holocaust.

There isn't a day when the camps don't flash across my mind. You can't escape, there is too much trauma. It is an ever-present thing - you can never forget. But I have always felt optimistic.

We did not lecture the children about what happened to our family during the war. But they knew a lot - they could tell by conversations and by the company we kept that great losses had taken place. The only thing you can hope for is that it will never happen to your children.

I am not religious - I go to synagogue only two or three times a year. But I believe in being Jewish and doing anything I can to help. Zionism was my first love and Israel is doing fine without us. But we still want to support Israel and we give financial assistance to Israelis from Iraq, Iran and the Yemen.

Sigo and I always did what we thought best. We always tried to be decent and kind. If we could help, we could. Our friends could rely on us and we on them. We have been lucky to be able to help others - it's a good feeling to have. If I had a message for future generations, I would say:

"Be an optimist. Stick to your principles and be proud of who your family is."

Sigo:

Before visiting Auschwitz, we travelled to Teschen. We went to visit a non-Jewish schoolmate called Gustav Kreinem. I did not recognise our family house - it had turned into a bus depot. The synagogue on the Czech side was an ordinary building with an inscription in Polish saying that a Jewish synagogue and centre had been here. This visit to my home town gave me nothing.

Next we travelled to Krakow in Poland where guided tours left everyday for Auschwitz. It was painful to see the railway which came right into the camp; so extremely neat and tidy now. I did not speak at all. I just watched and thought; deep private thoughts. I do not have to visit again but it was important to have made this journey. It was upsetting but sometimes you need to get upset. We had to make this pilgrimage to the place where our mothers died.

If I had to give a message to future generations I would say that human beings are born selfish - otherwise they could not survive - and unselfishness has to be acquired.

There are certain rules of behaviour established by religious or social movements which help develop unselfishness, and one ought to adopt such rules. I have always stuck to the rules, whether in soccer or socialism!

And I would also add: Always tell the truth.

Writer's Postscript

In the course of creating this book, Leah and Sigo Weber gave a significant amount of their time to tell me about their lives, delving deep to recall what were, at times, painful experiences. After I wrote a draft of these interviews, the Webers would check the copy for accuracy and check again as more information was added. I have stayed as faithful as possible to their original account, wanting to retain their turns of phrase and language. I hope that the reader hears Leah and Sigo's unique and vivid voices throughout. However, both were concerned to stress that much of what they recalled happened many decades ago. Consequently whilst what they have said is to the best of their recollection correct, there is always the possibility that, with the passage of time, memory might not be perfect.

One of the themes to emerge during the writing of this book was the creation of the State of Israel. In the light of the loss of family, friends and home, the Webers are acutely aware how the existence of a Jewish state may have prevented such suffering. Leah and Sigo Weber have worked tirelessly on behalf of the Zionist movement but, as modest people, they may not have told me all their achievements. Perhaps their contribution is best summed up by a guest at their recent Diamond Wedding celebration who repeated a remark made at a B'nai B'rith meeting: "This cannot be a committee meeting - neither of the Webers is here."

It was a privilege to meet Leah and Sigo Weber, who were always so helpful and gracious, and to share in their personal and often poignant memories. To hear the story of their lives has been a part of the process of remembering for the future. To bring their past to our awareness is an expression of hope that such terrible events may never happen again.

Elisabeth Winkler
August 2000

Glossary of Terms

Aliyah	Jewish emigration to Israel from the Diaspora
Barmitzvah	Coming of Age for a Jewish male - at the age of 13 years. An occasion which takes place in the synagogue and is accompanied by a celebration.
Brocha	Blessing made in Hebrew over food, wine and other appropriate things
Challah	Plaited bread used on the Sabbath table
Chalutz	Zionist pioneer in the Land of Israel
Chupah	A canopy, normally supported on 4 poles, beneath which a Jewish wedding ceremony takes place.
Cohen	A man descended from the priestly caste of Temple times. The *cohanim* (pl.) bless the congregation in synagogue.
Fleishig	Meat. Not to be mixed with dairy products, as prescribed in laws relating to kosher food *(Yiddish)*
Frum	Orthodox in practice *(Yiddish)*
Hagana	Jewish defence force in pre-State Israel
Habonim	A secular Zionist Youth Group - now known as *Habonim Dror.*
Hachshara	Training camp for prospective kibbutz farmers, prior to the establishment of the State of Israel in 1948
Hechalutz	The *Chalutz* Organising Body
Ivrit	Modern Hebrew, as spoken in Israel
Kaftan	Long black coat traditionally worn by strictly orthodox Jewish men *(Yiddish)*
Ketuba	Jewish marriage contract
Kibbutz	Pioneer collective settlement in Israel
Kiddush	A reception with wine held after a religious celebration
Kosher	Suitable for consumption according to Jewish dietary laws

Maftir   A portion read from the Torah scroll by the barmitzvah boy in Synagogue

Milshig   Dairy food. Not to be mixed with meat, as prescribed in laws on kosher food *(Yiddish)*

Minyan   A quorum of 10 Jewish males over the age of barmitzvah (13 years), necessary to perform certain prayers and religious rituals

Mohel   Man who performs circumcisions on Jewish baby boys

Shabbat   The Jewish Sabbath

Shadchen   One who introduces Jewish men and women to one another for possible marriage *(Yiddish)*

Sheitl   Wig worn by orthodox Jewish married women to conceal their hair *(Yiddish)*

Shivah   Jewish ritual of mourning i.e 'sitting shivah'

Shmaltz   Rendered chicken or goose fat *(Yiddish)*

Stiebl   A small house of prayer in the Eastern European tradition *(Yiddish)*

Tefillin   Phylacteries *(Greek)*. Black leather boxes containing tiny scrolls attached to black leather straps. Worn at prayer by adult Jewish males

Torah Scroll The Five Books of Moses, hand written on a parchment scroll by a scribe and read in the synagogue on Sabbath, festivals and other occasions

Tref   Non-kosher meat or fish

Tsorres   Troubles or problems *(Yiddish)*